NeoWhimsies

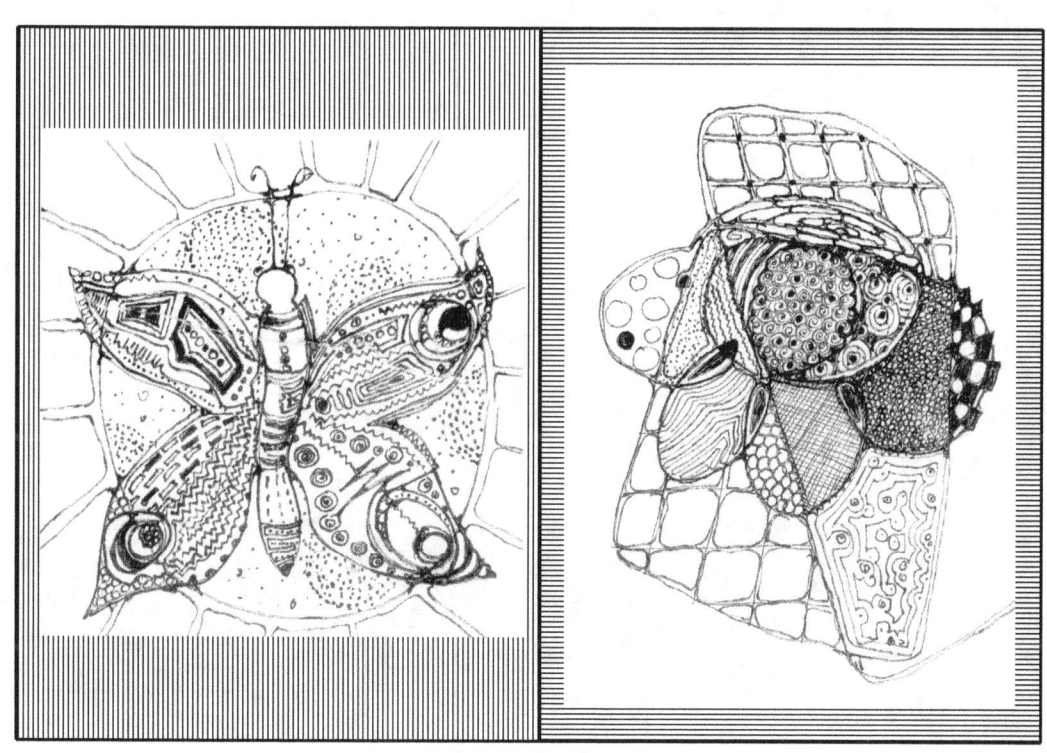

NEOPOPREALISM

ink drawing basics
FOR MANNEQUINS

Illustrated by **Nadia RUSS**
NeoPopRealismPRESS

A book "NeoWhimsies: NeoPopReaism Ink Drawing Basics for Mannequins" by NeoPopRealism PRESS invites the readers on an enlightening journey to the imaginative and whimsical world of NeoWhimsies. It will help you develop imagination and sense of composition.

NeoWhimsies

NeoPopRealism

ink drawing basics
for MANNEQUINS

NeoPopRealismPRESS

First published in 2012 by NeoPopRealism PRESS
PO BOX 366
New York, NY 10013

NeopoprealismPress@mail.com

"NeoWhimsies: NeoPopRealism Ink Drawing Basics for Mannequins" by NeoPopRealism PRESS
Illustrated by Nadia Russ

Published in the United States of America
Language: English

ISBN-13: 978-0615651859
ISBN-10: 0615651852

12 13 14 15 16   10 9 8 7 6 5 4 3 2 1

This book teaches children and artisans how to draw NeoWhimsies - the simplified NeoPopRealism ink images.
www.neopoprealism.org

CONTENT

INTRODUCTION

NeoPopRealism art style and ink drawing concept was created by artist Nadia Russ in 1989. It was an experiment. She was trying to connect to the Universe and let the Universe use her as a conductor when she created her drawings. She didn't want to follow any other artists' achievements, she decided to create absolutely new art form, like Picasso (Cubism), Dali (Surrealism), Andy Warhol (Pop Art) and a few other worldwide known artists had done. Nadia Russ took her ink pen and began to draw a flowing line, which turned into shapes, figures, often faces. Then, some sections (or all), which appeared, she filled with the repetitive patterns. She never uses eraser because if a mistake made, it disappears with the following repetitive patterns that balance the whole composition. Her work was unique, no one did anything like this before.

Later, January 4, 2003, Nadia Russ created a word NeoPopRealism and internationally announced new style of visual arts. Today, her artwork can be found in the private, corporate and museums' art collections worldwide. She lives in the U.S.

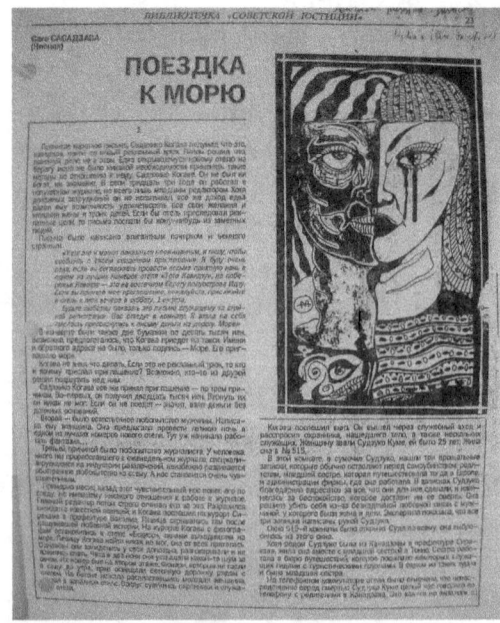

Nadia Russ illustrated a story by Saho Sasadzava for the *Russian Justice* Journal, 1992, Moscow, Russia

Get INSPIRED

Creating requires Inspiration. When you focus on your success, you fall into the trap of comparing yourself to other people, feeling envious. Instead, focus on getting better every day. Focus on excellence. Use your strengths for a bigger purpose beyond yourself. Focus on what you are giving instead of what you are getting, it makes every your step more rewarding and meaningful.

Get the black ink pen *Foray Rolle Rollerball Medium 0.7 mm* or *Sharpie* and a piece of cardstock paper 8.5"x11". Cut it into two pieces - 5.5"x8.5" each. Now, you need one piece.

You would like to create something very unique and that's not always easy to do. You need to learn how to connect to the Universe and open your mind to the higher powers.

Close your eyes for a moment. Imaging that your consciousness leaves and fly to the Space where there are no people but only super speed and super powers. Forget about your daily life experiences. No noise should disturb you except, possible, music. You are not you any more; you are a part of the Universe.

Slowly open your eyes. Try not to look around, look only at your piece of the plain white paper. This is the beginning. . . Now draw.

If you after all couldn't draw the NeoPopRealism image, go to the next pages of this book. After you learn how to draw with the all offered tips and tricks, come back to this page again and let see what will happen.

This book will teach you how to draw NeoWhimsies. NeoWhimsies are the simple NeoPopRealism ink drawings. This book is filled with NeoWhimsies! Learn how to draw NeoWhimsies and you will be able to create more complicated, the NeoPopRealism artwork and exhibit it in the art galleries.

Draw the Eggs

Next pages will show you how to create step-by-step NeoWhimsies Eggs.

NeoWhimsy is a simplified NeoPopRealism ink drawing, made out of line and combination of sections filled with the imaginative patterns. Each drawing - NeoWhimsy - has different character. The following visual instructions will lead you from the beginning to end of the drawing process. Every following image includes new detail(s). The final NeoWhimsies look like the following:

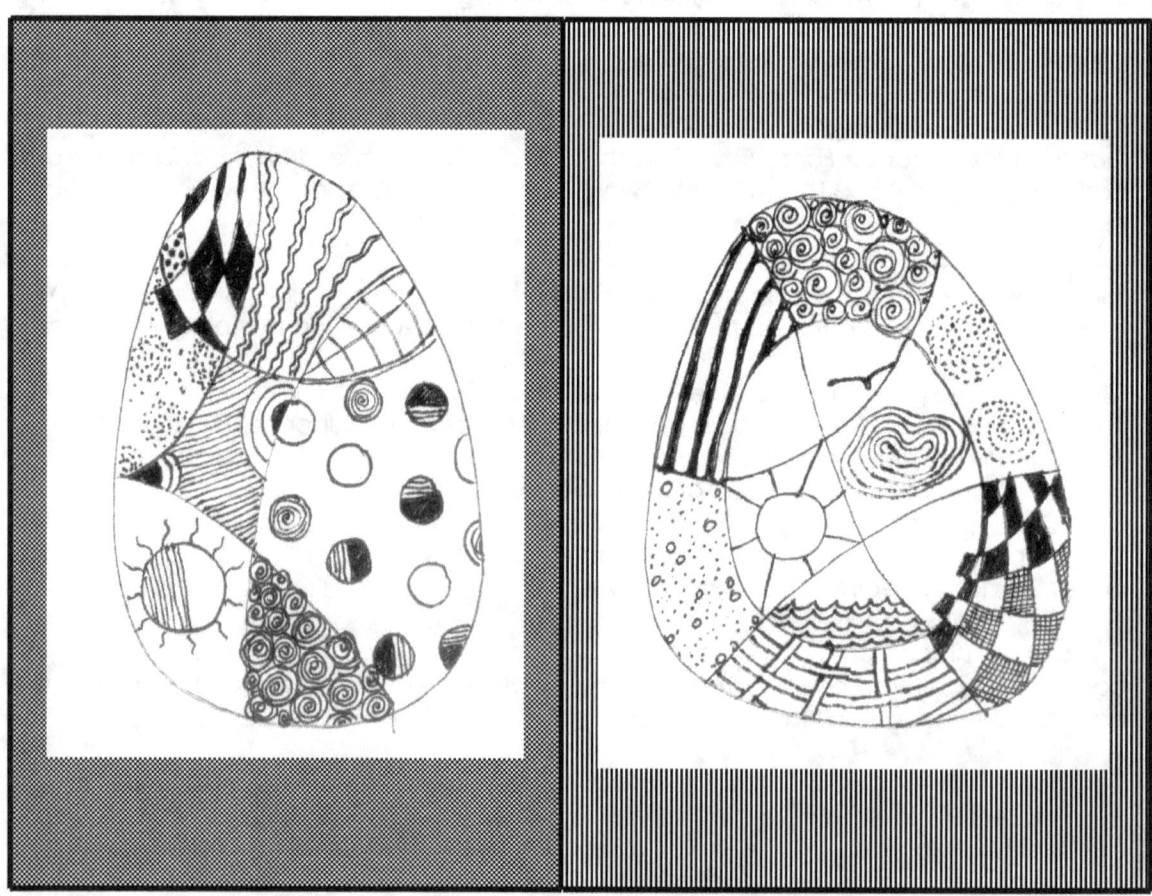

Egg 1   Egg 2

How to Draw Egg 1

Before you start to draw NeoWhimsy *Egg 1,* learn how to draw the patterns used in this drawing. You will find them below.

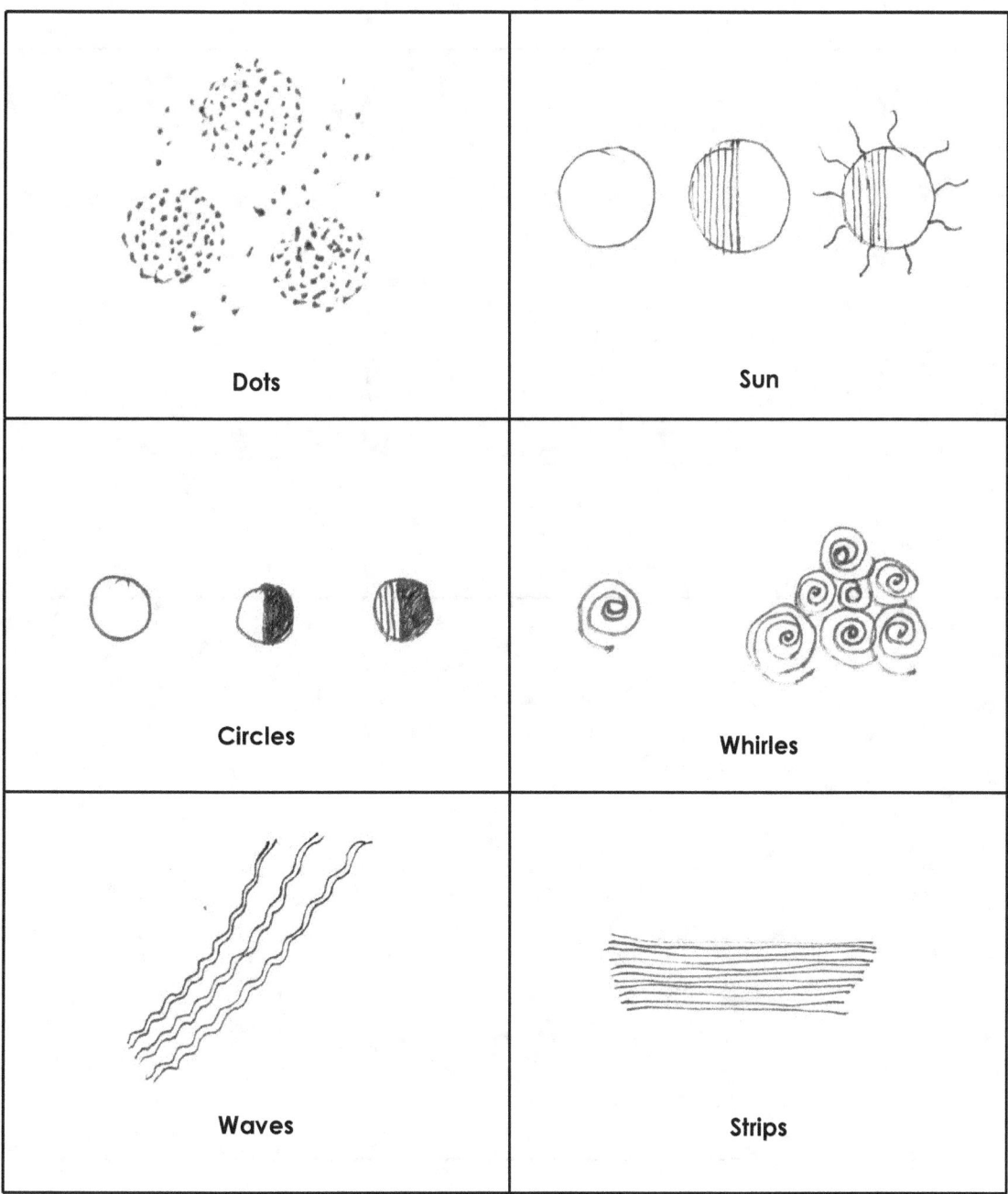

Dots

Sun

Circles

Whirles

Waves

Strips

The following pages will teach you step-by-step how to draw NeoWhimsy Egg 1. You will learn how to draw the flowing line - a contour, how to divide an image into the sections, and then, how to fill these sections with patterns, making your egg look whimsical and artistic. When you create your NeoWhimsies you develop your imagination and artistic skills.

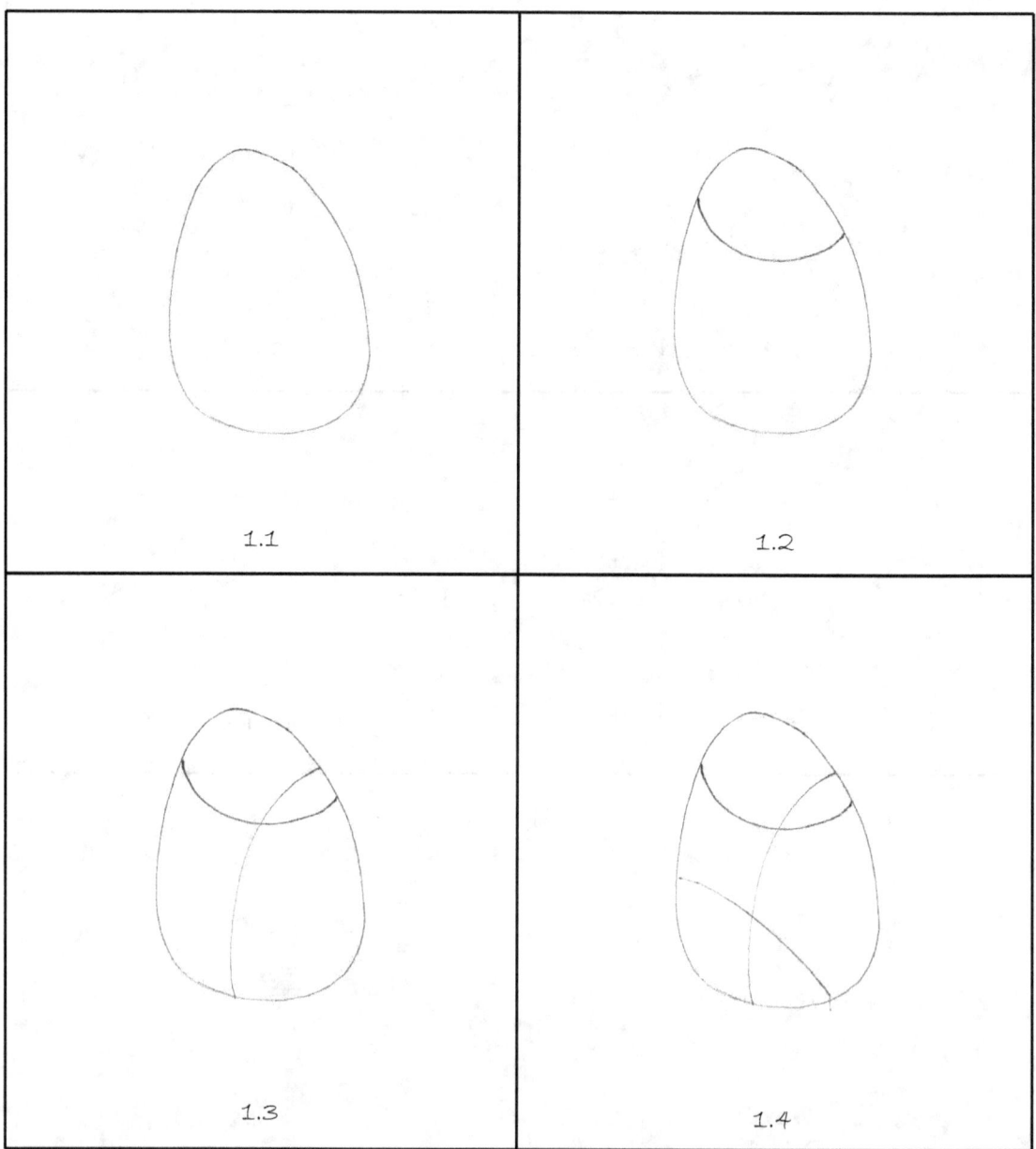

1.1

1.2

1.3

1.4

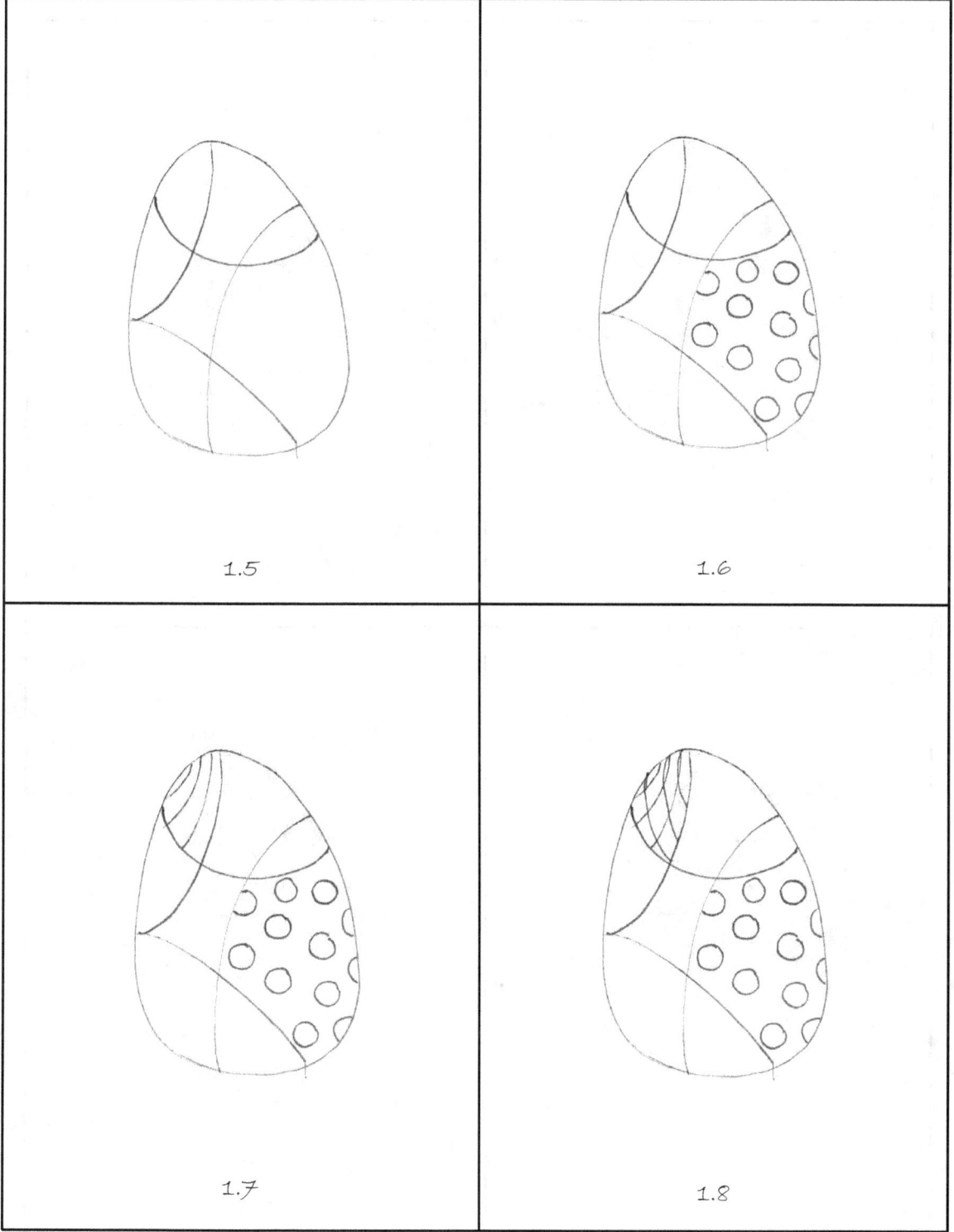

1.5

1.6

1.7

1.8

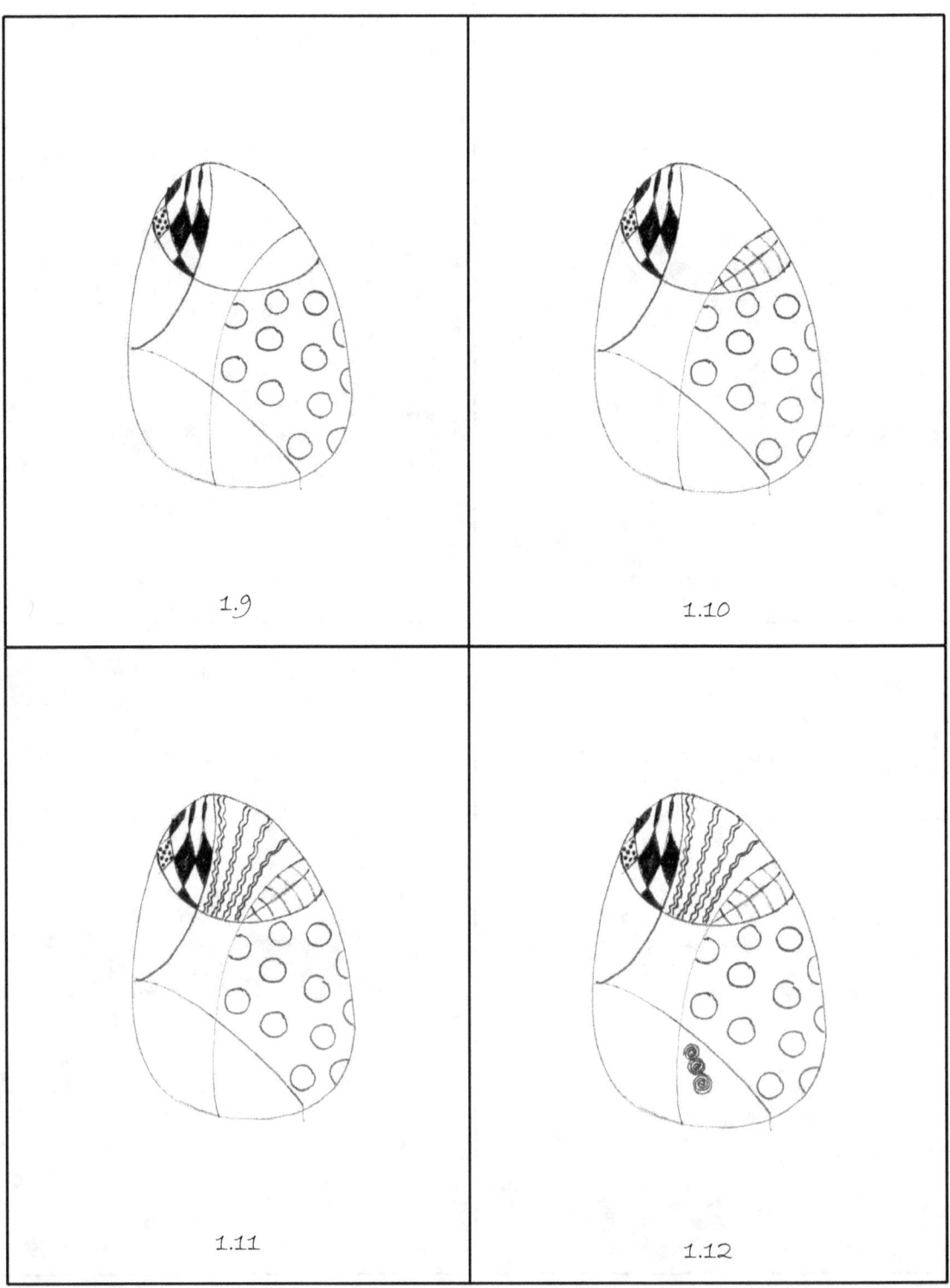

1.9

1.10

1.11

1.12

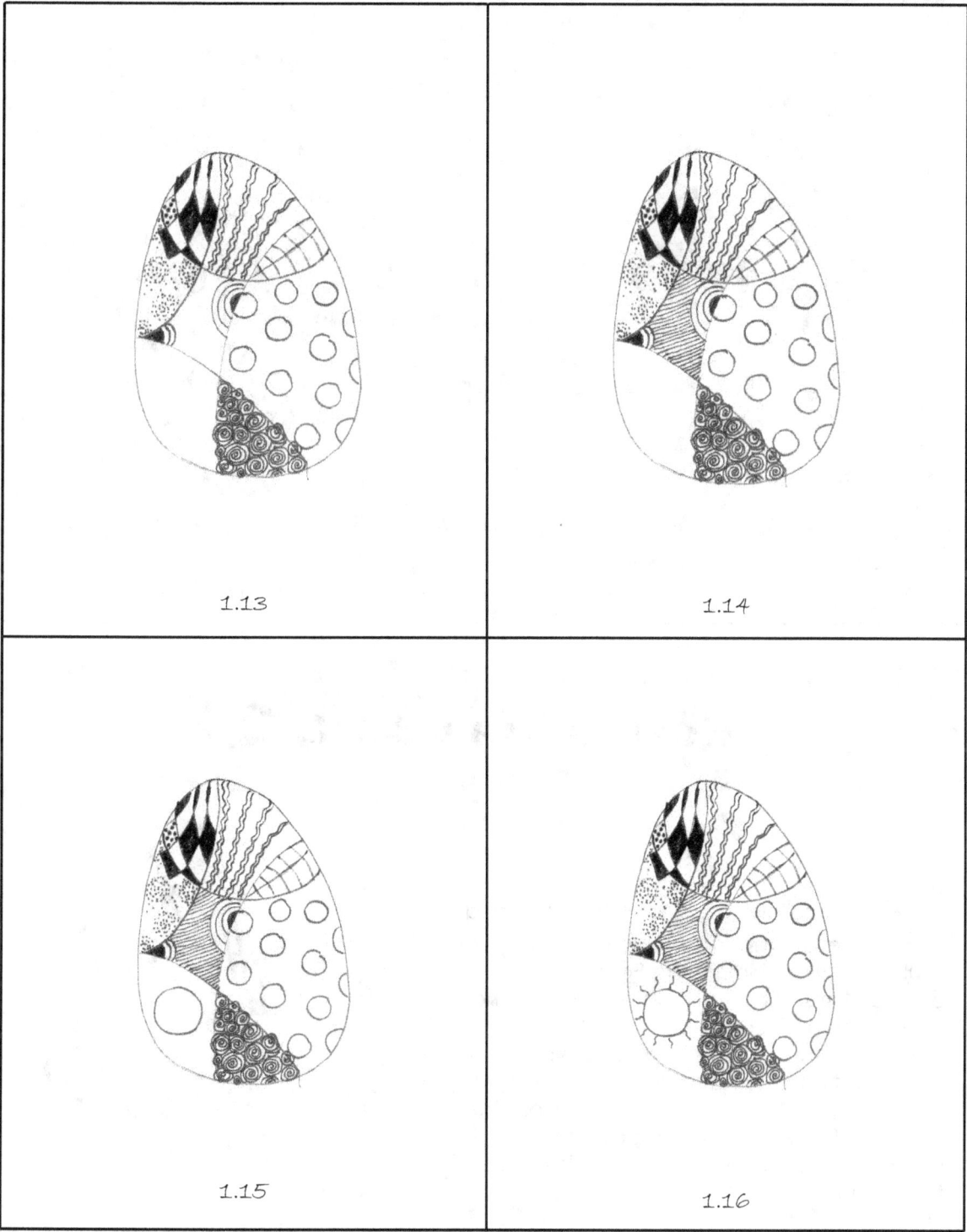

1.13

1.14

1.15

1.16

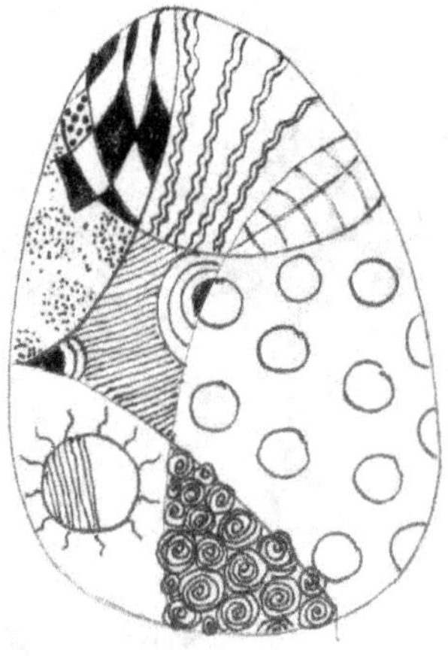

1.17

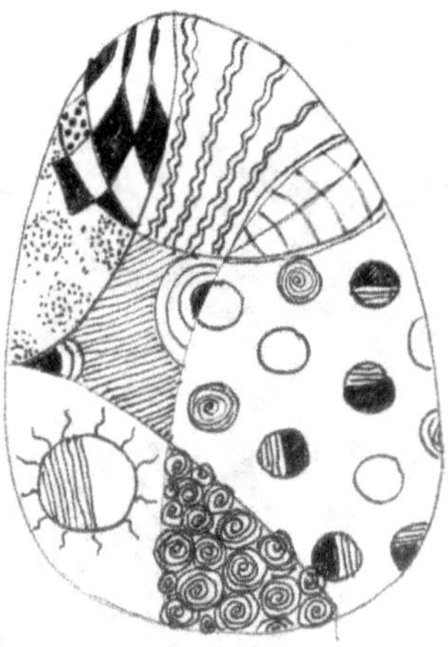

1.18

How to Draw Egg 2

Follow the following visual instructions and you will be able to learn how to create the exuberant NeoWhimsies like Egg 2. An image of NeoWhimsy Egg 2 is imaginative. Do not worry if you make a mistake; you do not have to erase it. It will "disappears" after you draw more patterns, because these patterns will balance the entire composition of the drawing. The sense of composition in art is very important sense and can be developed through the training.

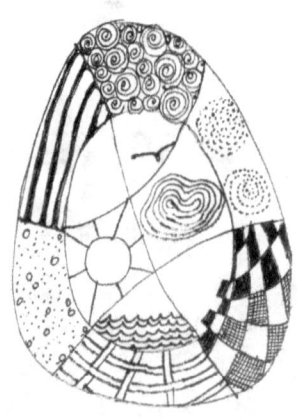

The Egg 2

Before you start to draw NeoWhimsy The Egg 2, learn how to draw the patterns, used in this drawing.

Dots' Whirle	**Whirles**	**Breeze**
Cloud	**Sun**	**Strips**
Chess board	**Dots with Circles**	

Follow the visual Instructions and you will be able to create beautiful NeoWhimsies.

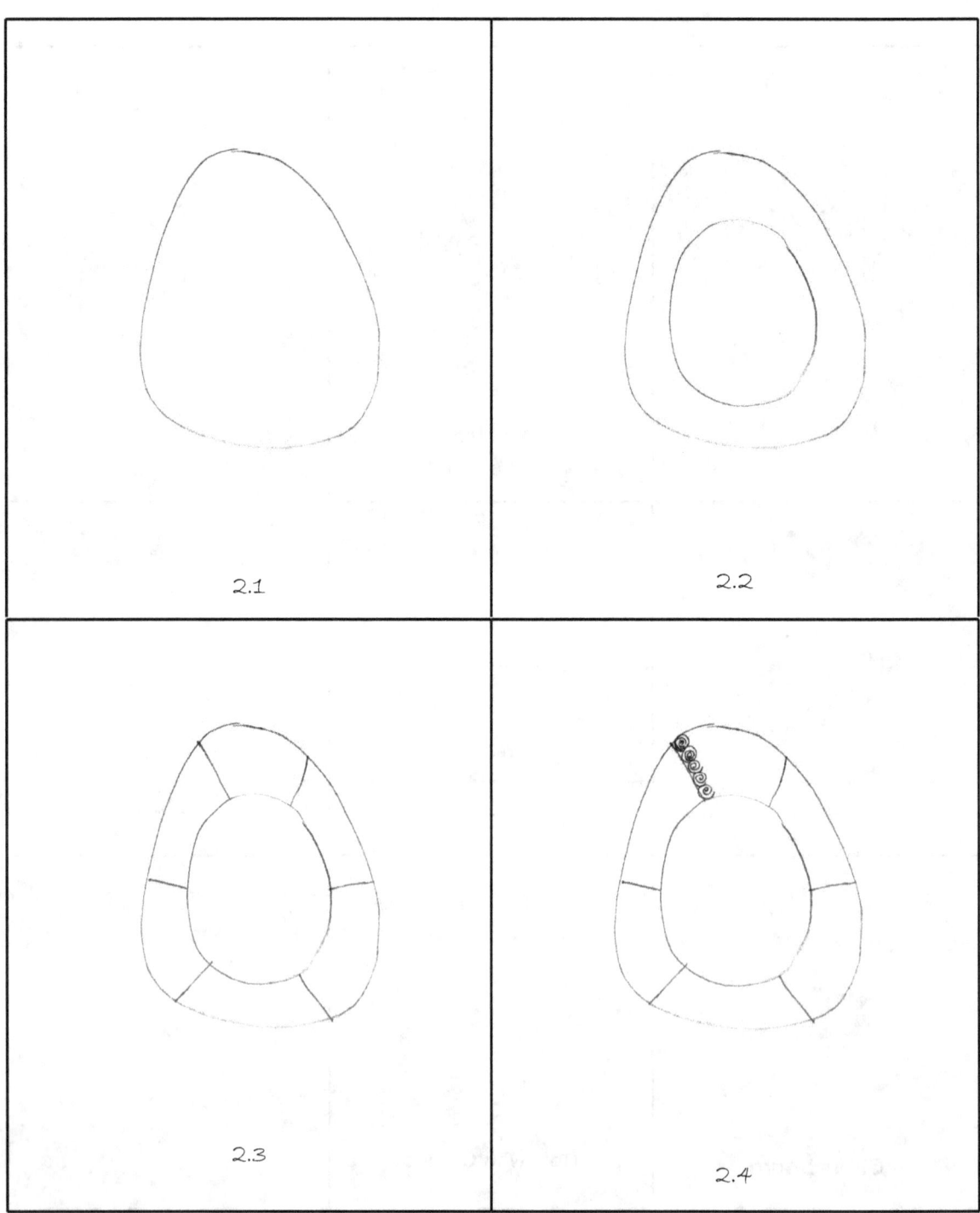

2.1

2.2

2.3

2.4

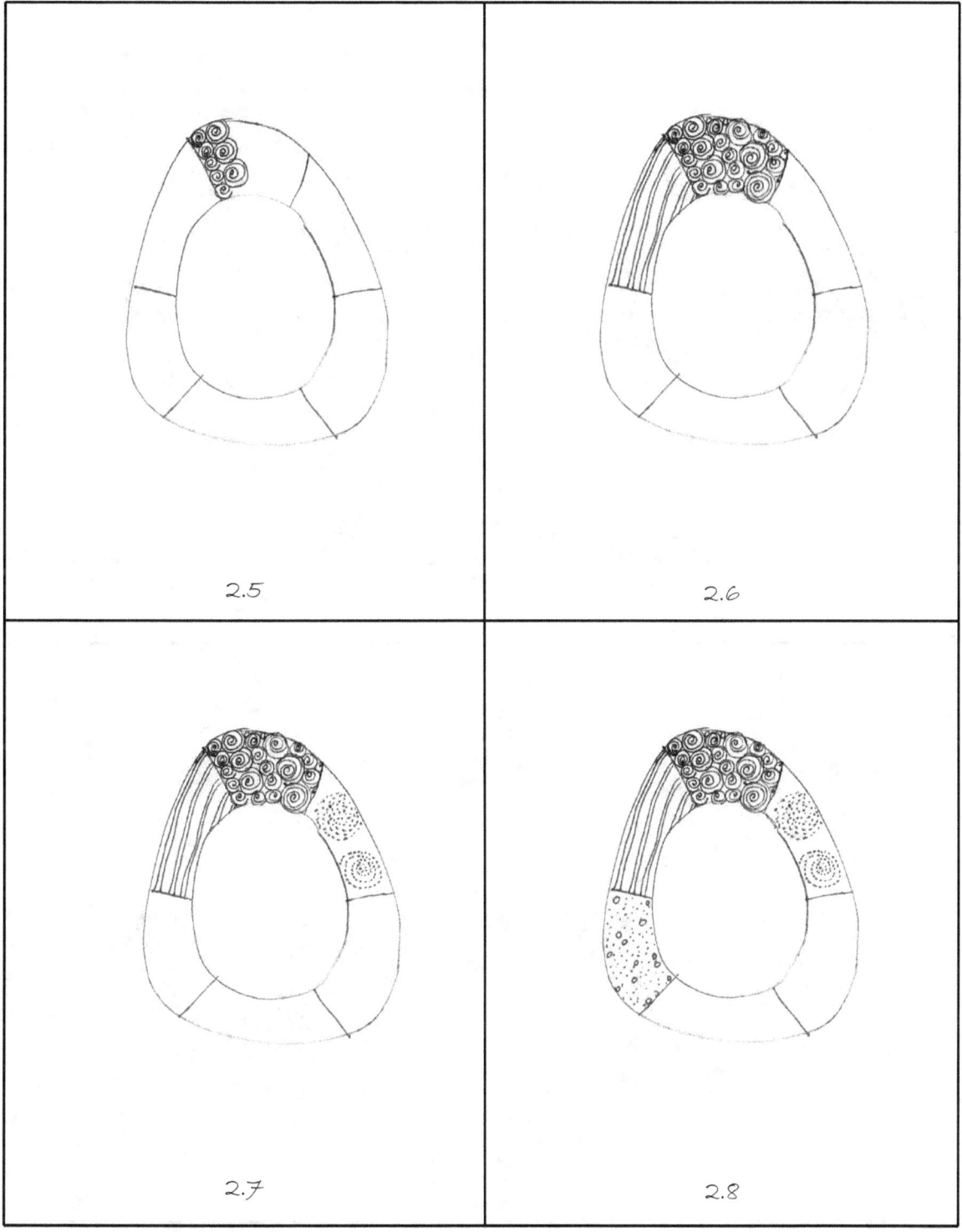

2.5

2.6

2.7

2.8

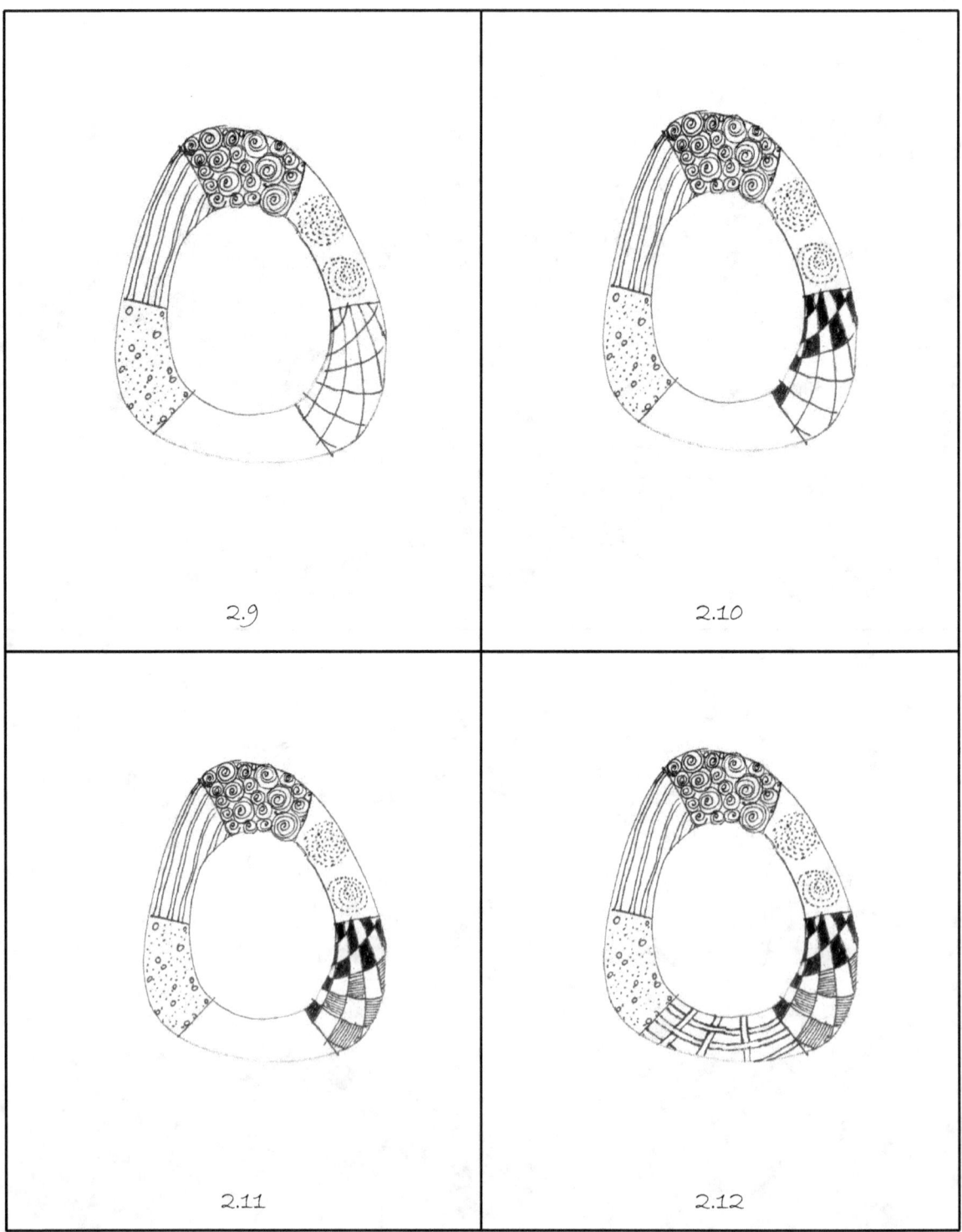

2.9

2.10

2.11

2.12

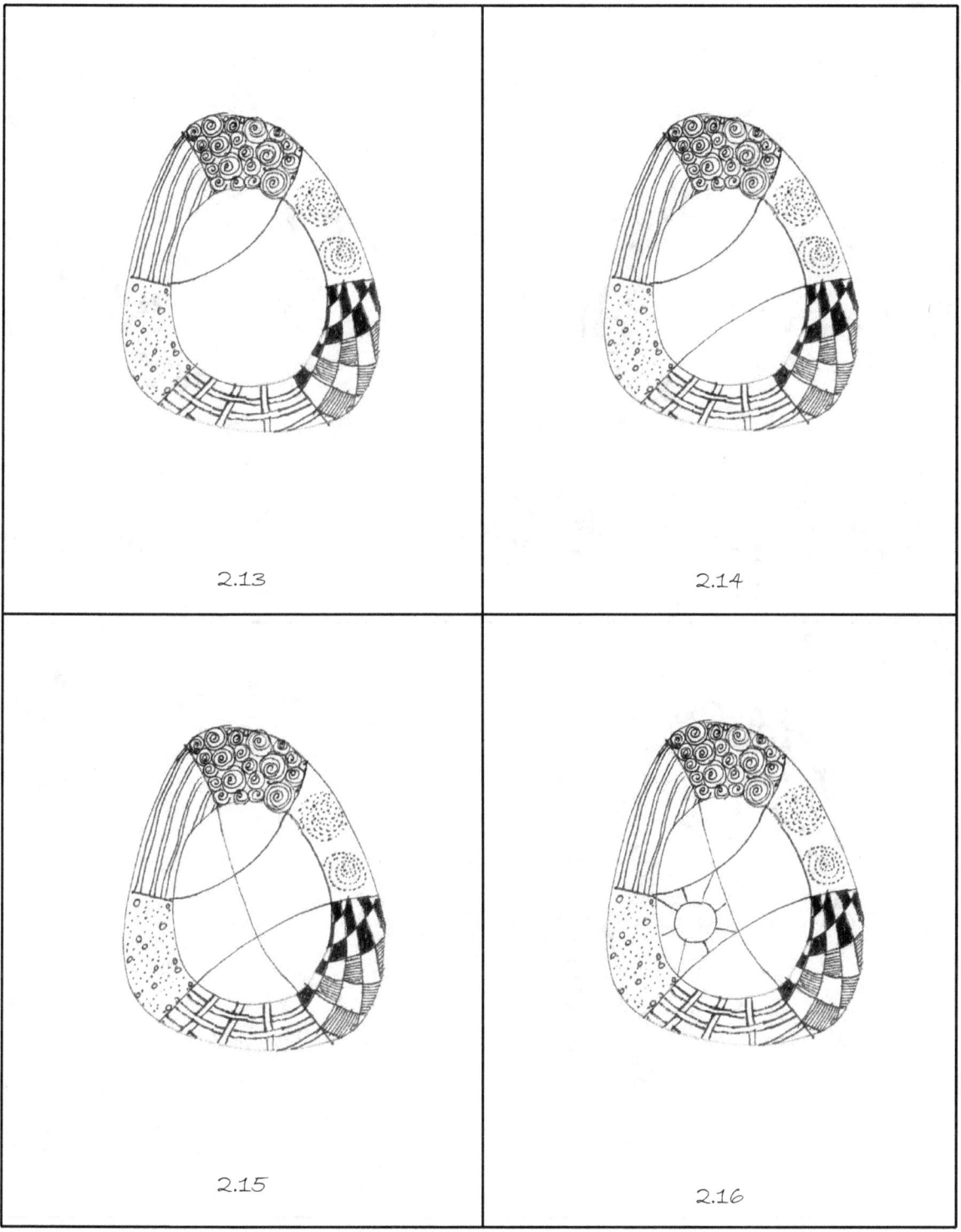

2.13

2.14

2.15

2.16

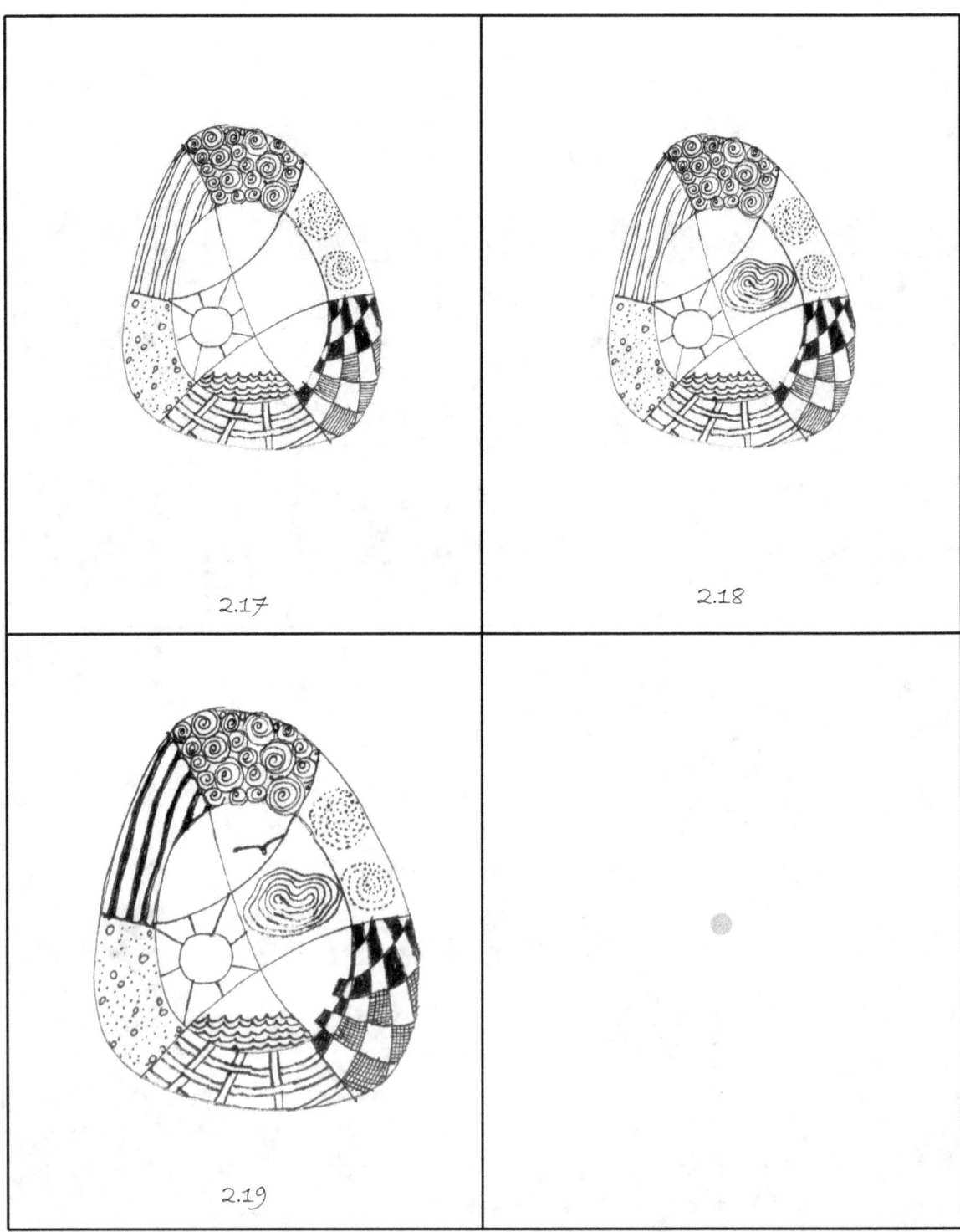

2.17

2.18

2.19

Draw the **Eggs** Here and Now

Use the following pages for your training. Get your ink pen and fill sections of the eggs with different repetitive patterns. Create patterns using your imagination, follow your creative instinct. Some section(s) leave blank. When you draw, you enter the meditative state of mind. There is a deep connection between meditation, health, and happiness. The drawing helps experience calm and peace of mind, it increases your energy and vitality. More you practice, better you skills and Imagination are. Imagination is a very important artistic quality; it is considered a power of the mind, a creative faculty of the mind, and the mind itself when in use. It is a process of the mind used for thinking, creating, fantasizing, more. More you practice, better your results are.

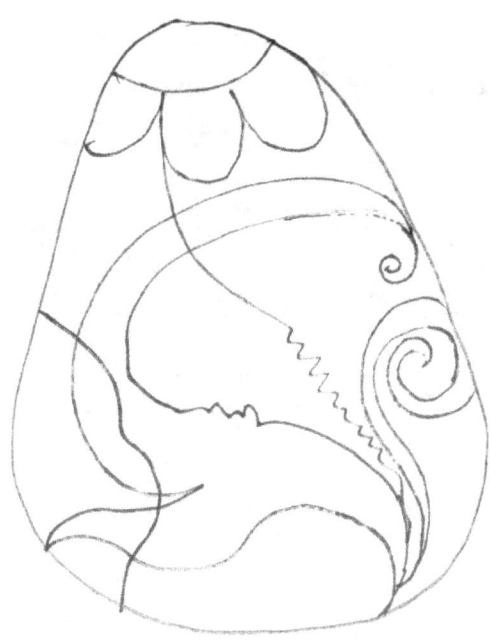

The Egg 1

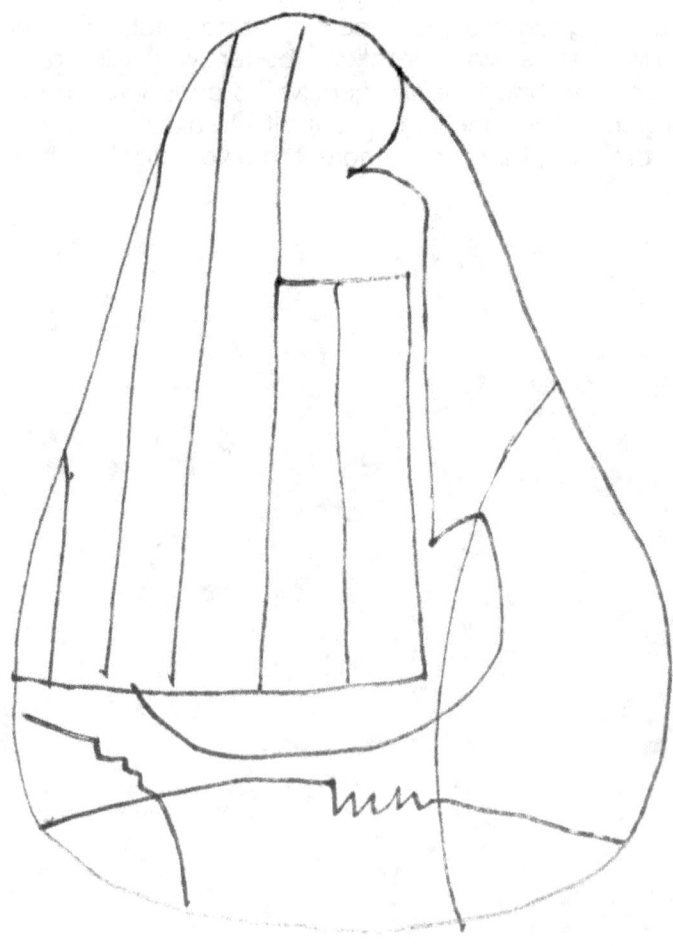

The Egg 2

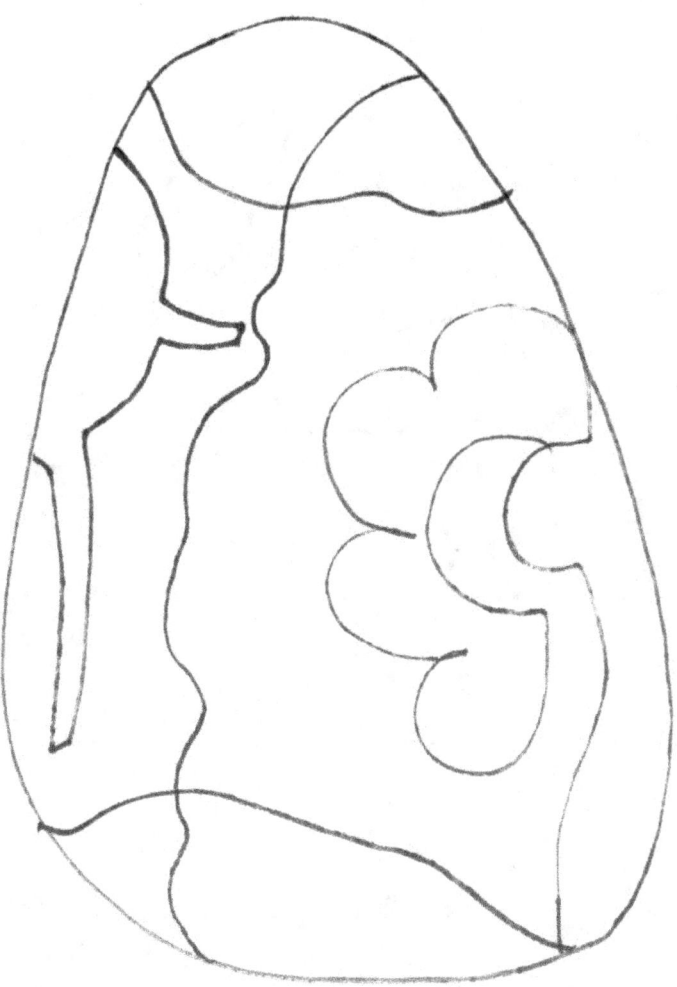

The Egg 3

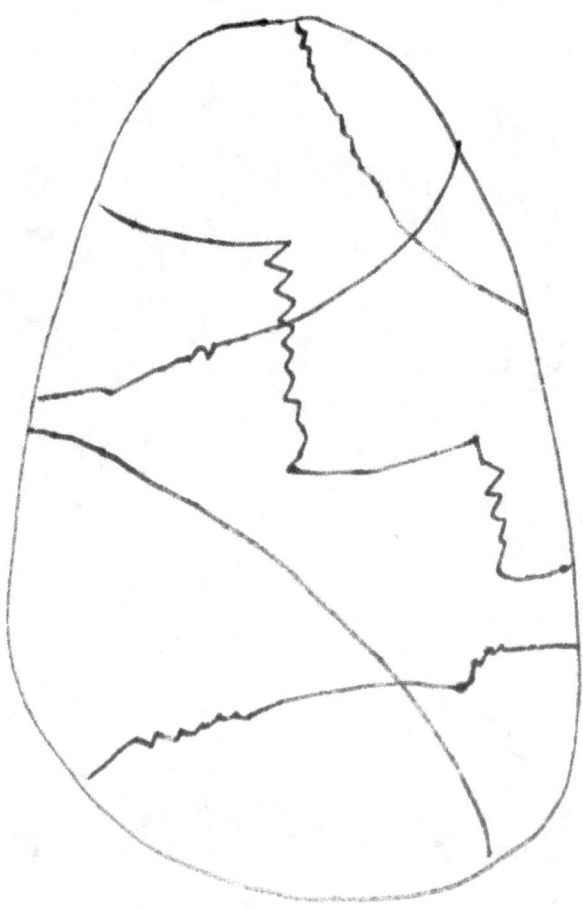

The Egg 4

Draw the Butterflies

The following pages will show you how to create step-by-step the Butterflies. These NeoWhimsies made out of line and patterns. The visual instructions will lead you through the entire drawing process from the beginning to end. Every following image includes new detail(s). The final images look like these:

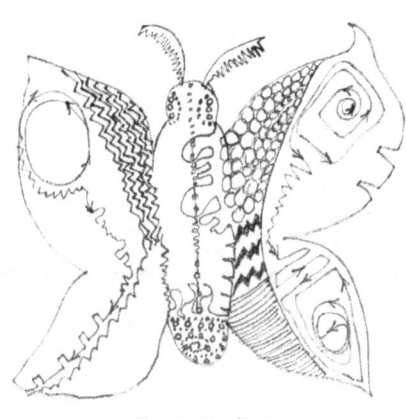

The Butterfly 1

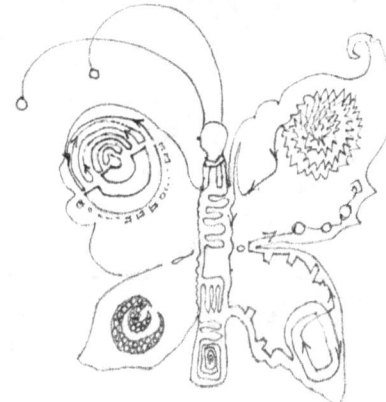

The Butterfly 2

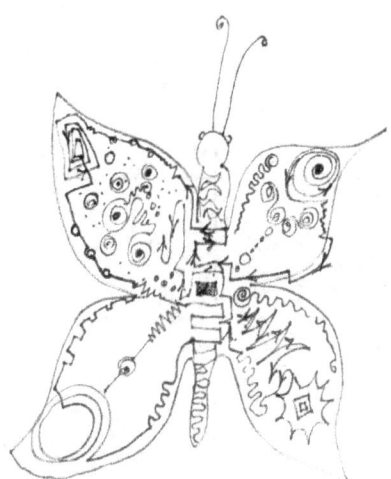

The Butterfly 3

How to Draw Butterfly 1

This page includes the patterns, used in NeoWhimsy Butterfly 1.

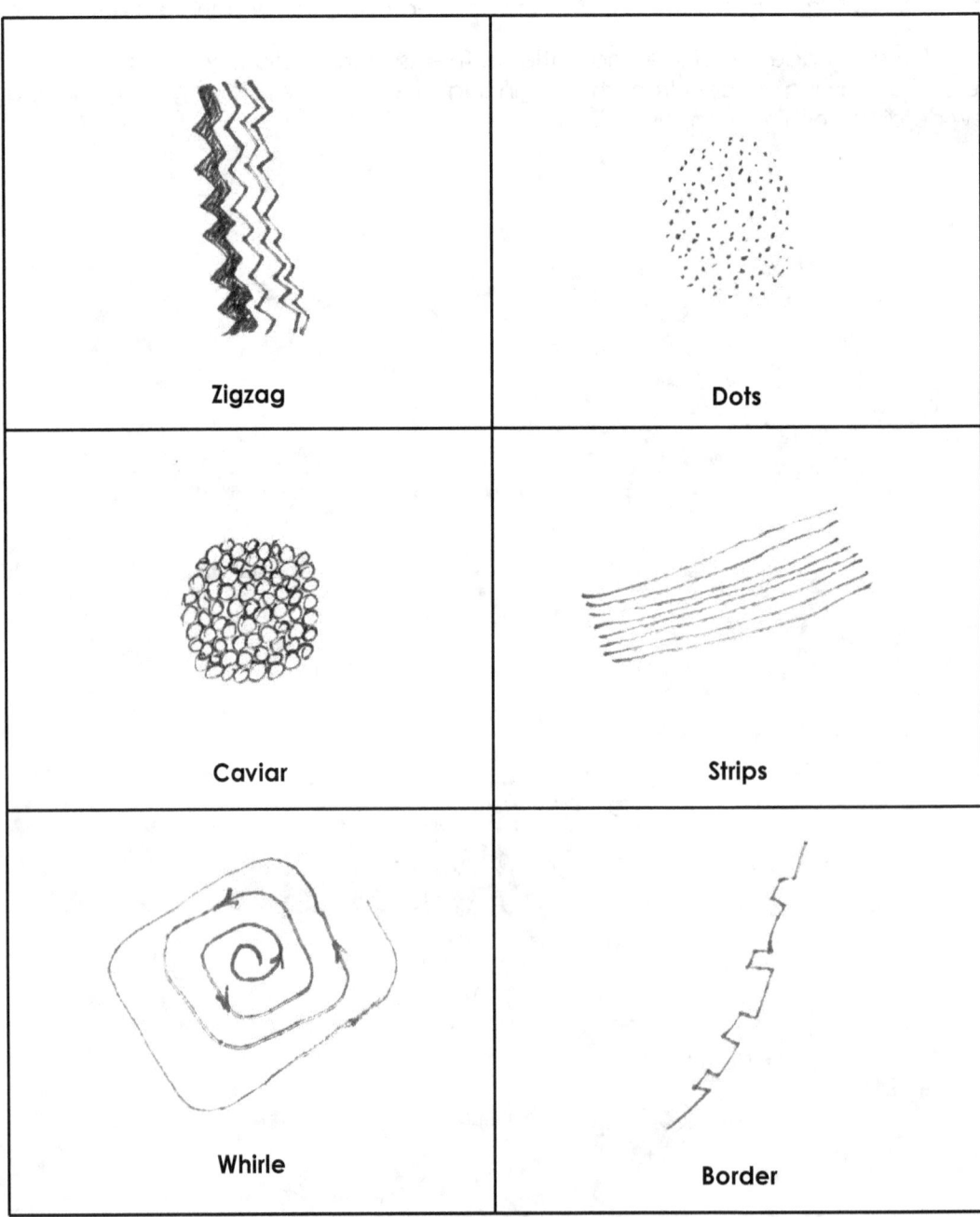

Zigzag	**Dots**
Caviar	**Strips**
Whirle	**Border**

The following pages show step by step how to create NeoWhimsy Butterfly 1. Follow the visual instructions and learn how to create the whimsical images. When you'll understand the process of the image developing, you will be able to create the images on your own. Free your mind, get creative!

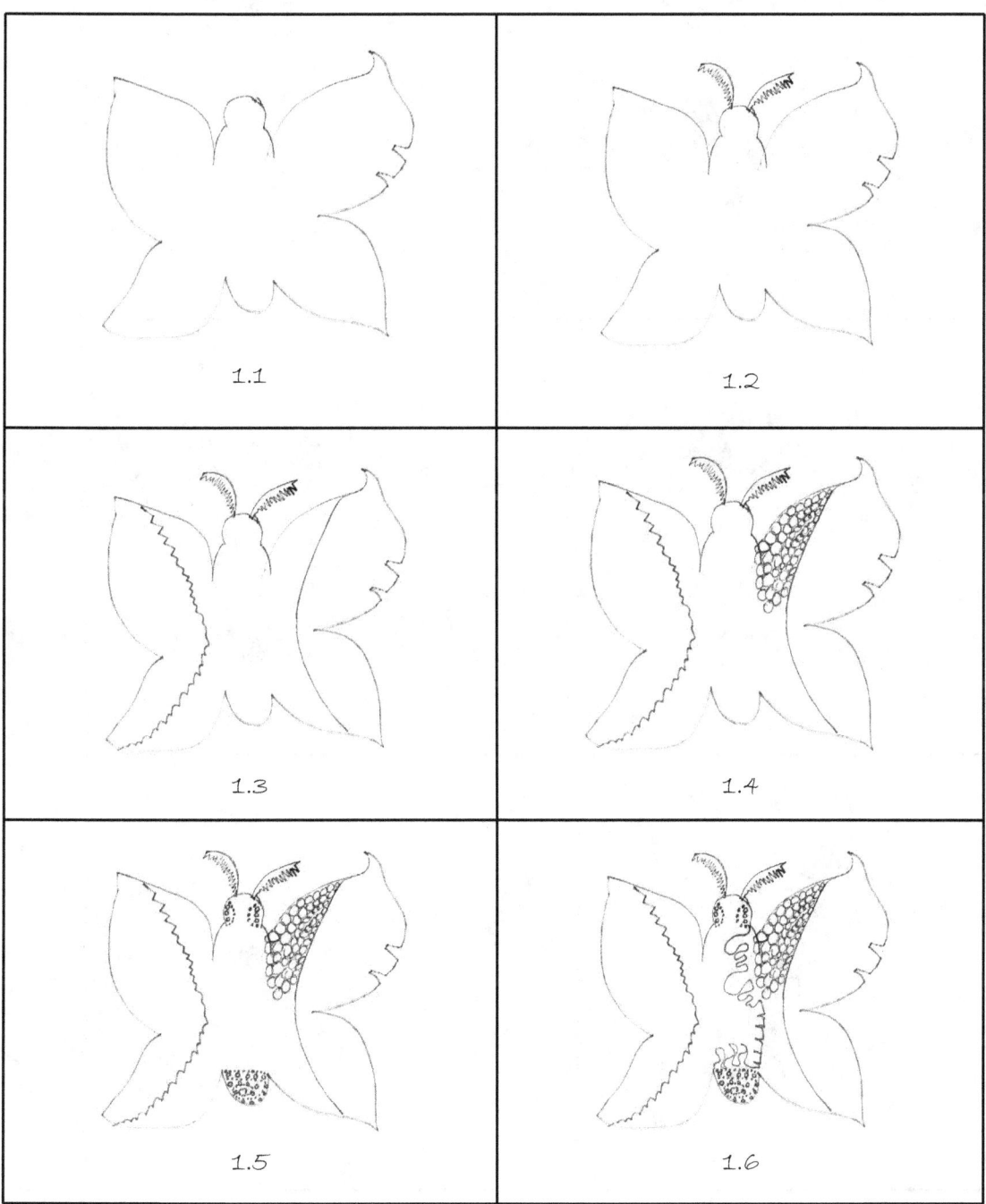

1.1

1.2

1.3

1.4

1.5

1.6

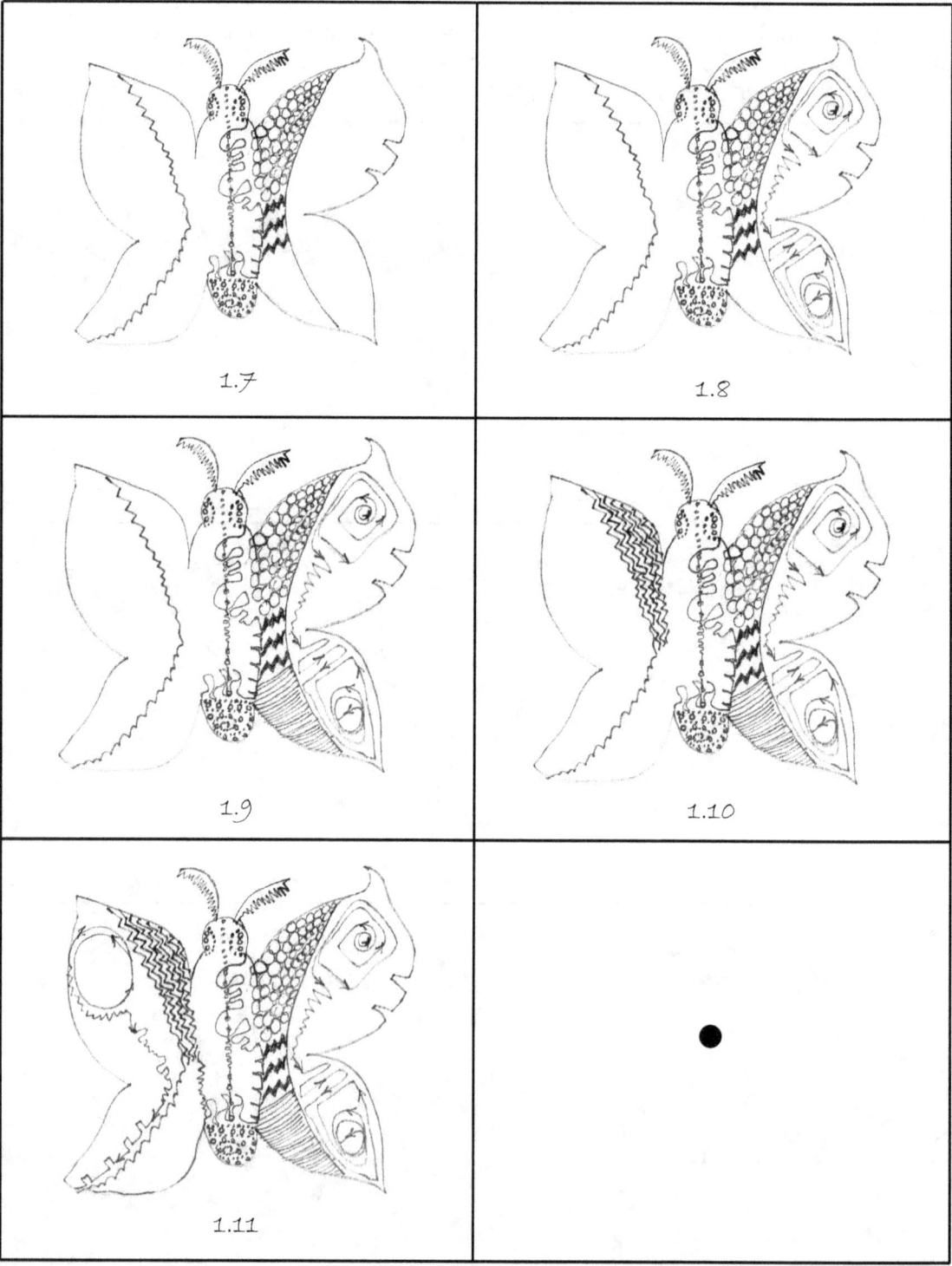

1.7

1.8

1.9

1.10

1.11

The NeoWhimsies look beautiful when they are framed.

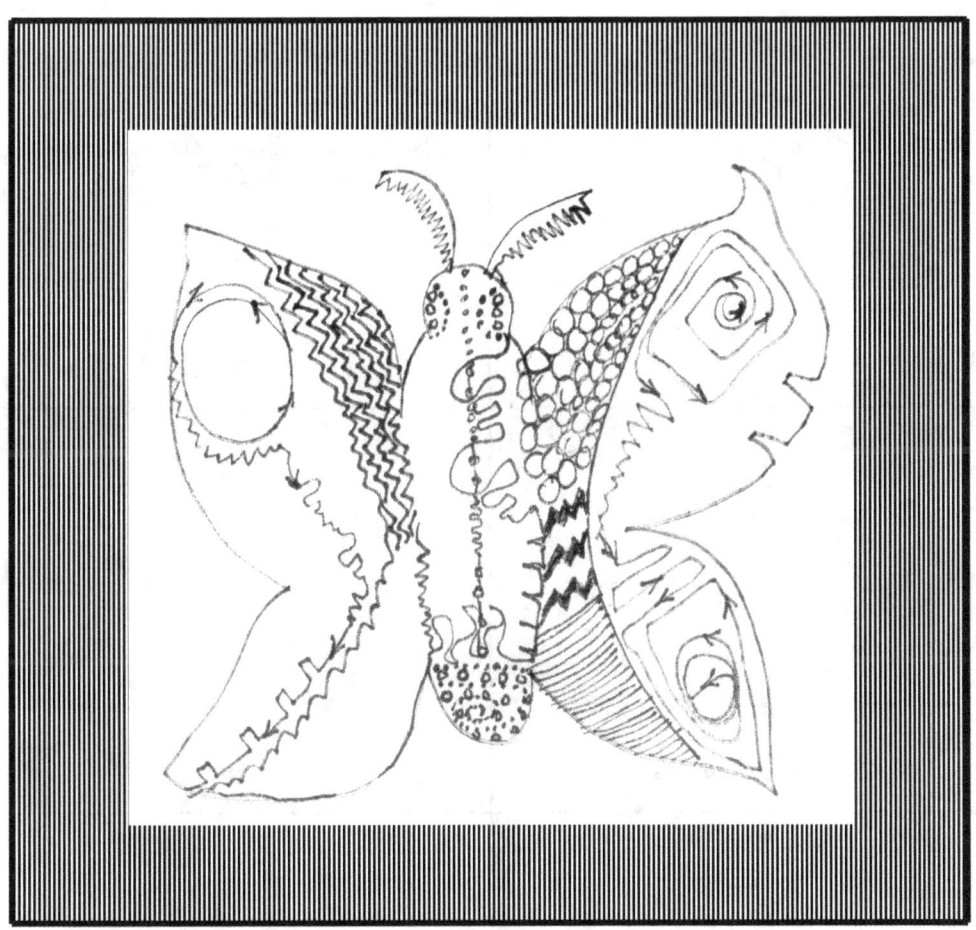

The Butterfly 1

How to Draw Butterfly 2

This page includes the repetitive patterns' samples, used in NeoWhimsy Butterfly 2.

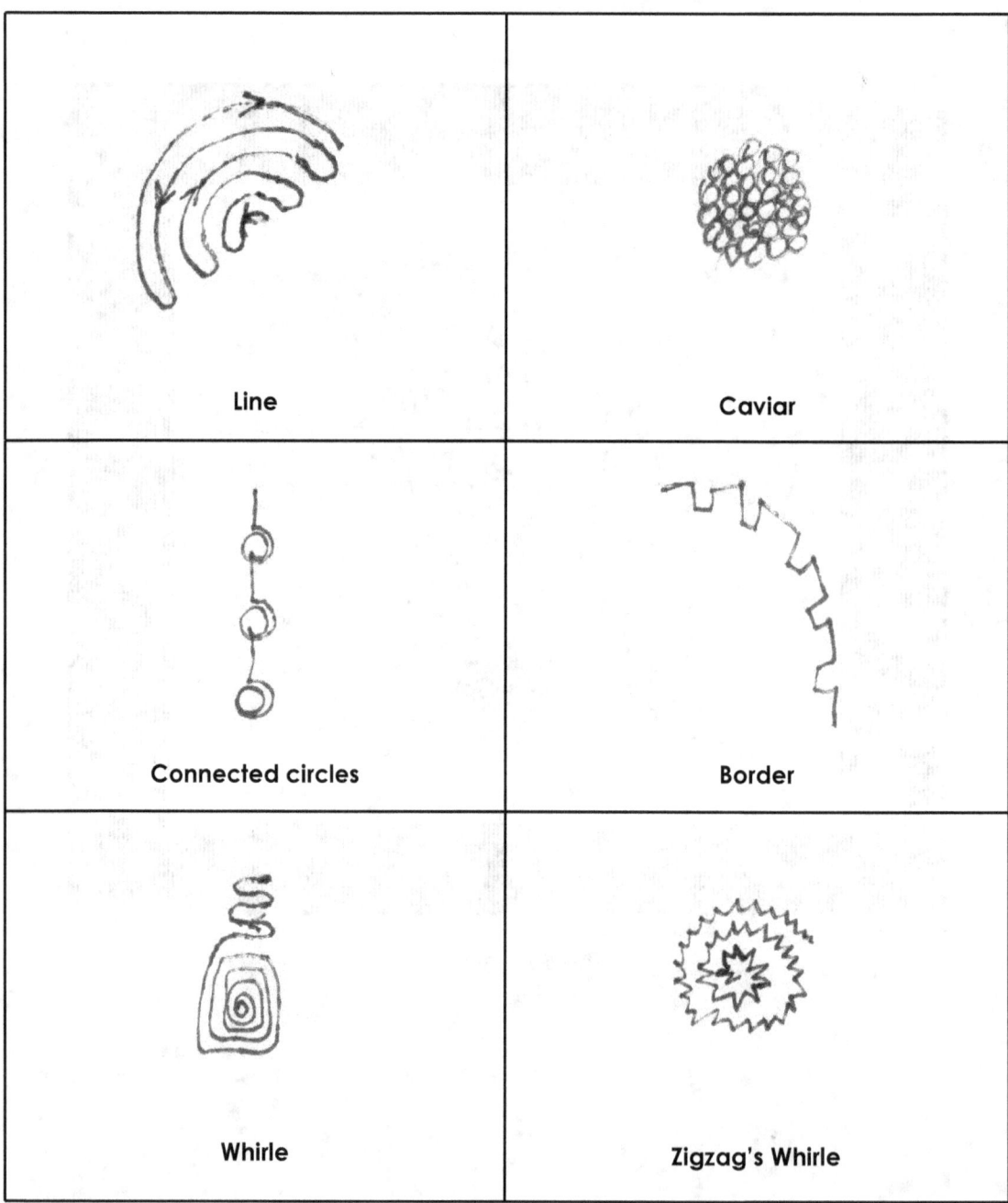

Line	**Caviar**
Connected circles	**Border**
Whirle	**Zigzag's Whirle**

Next pages will show you how to create NeoWhimsy Butterfly 2. Follow the visual instructions and you will be able to create different NeoWhimsies on your own.

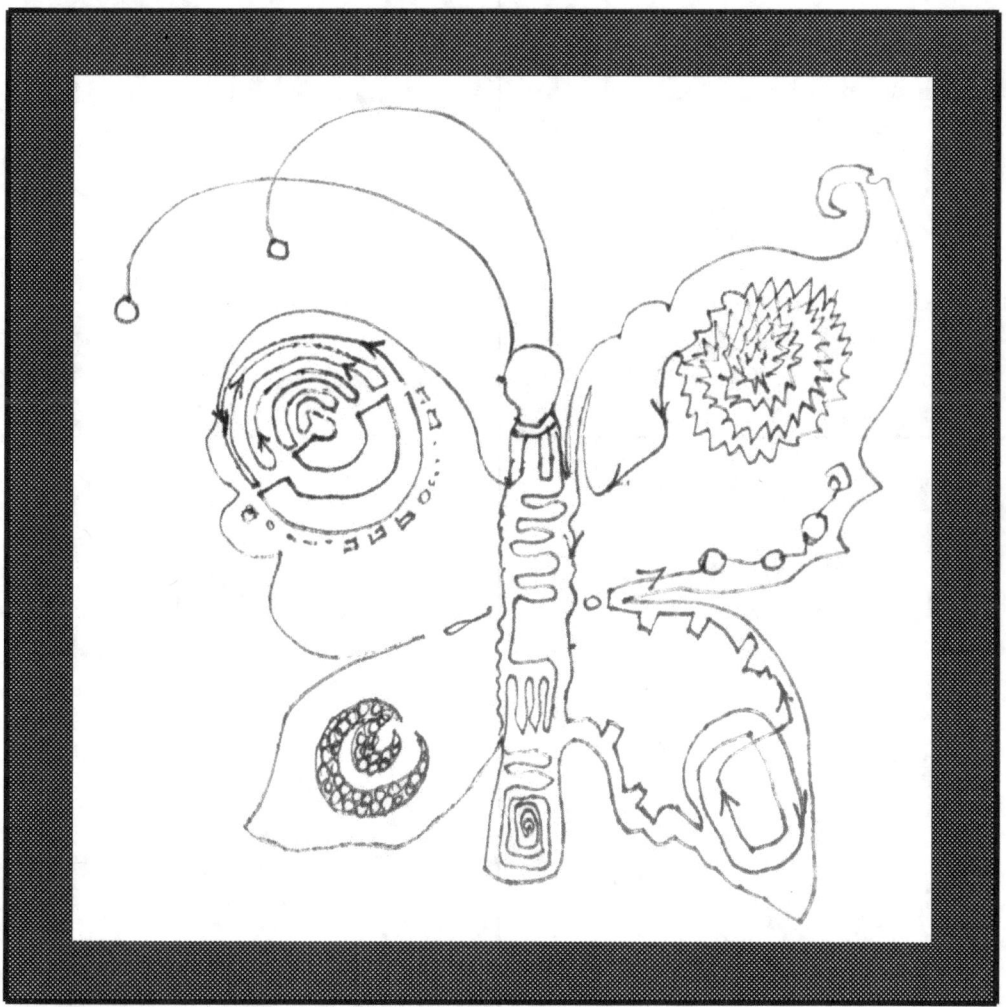

The Butterfly 2

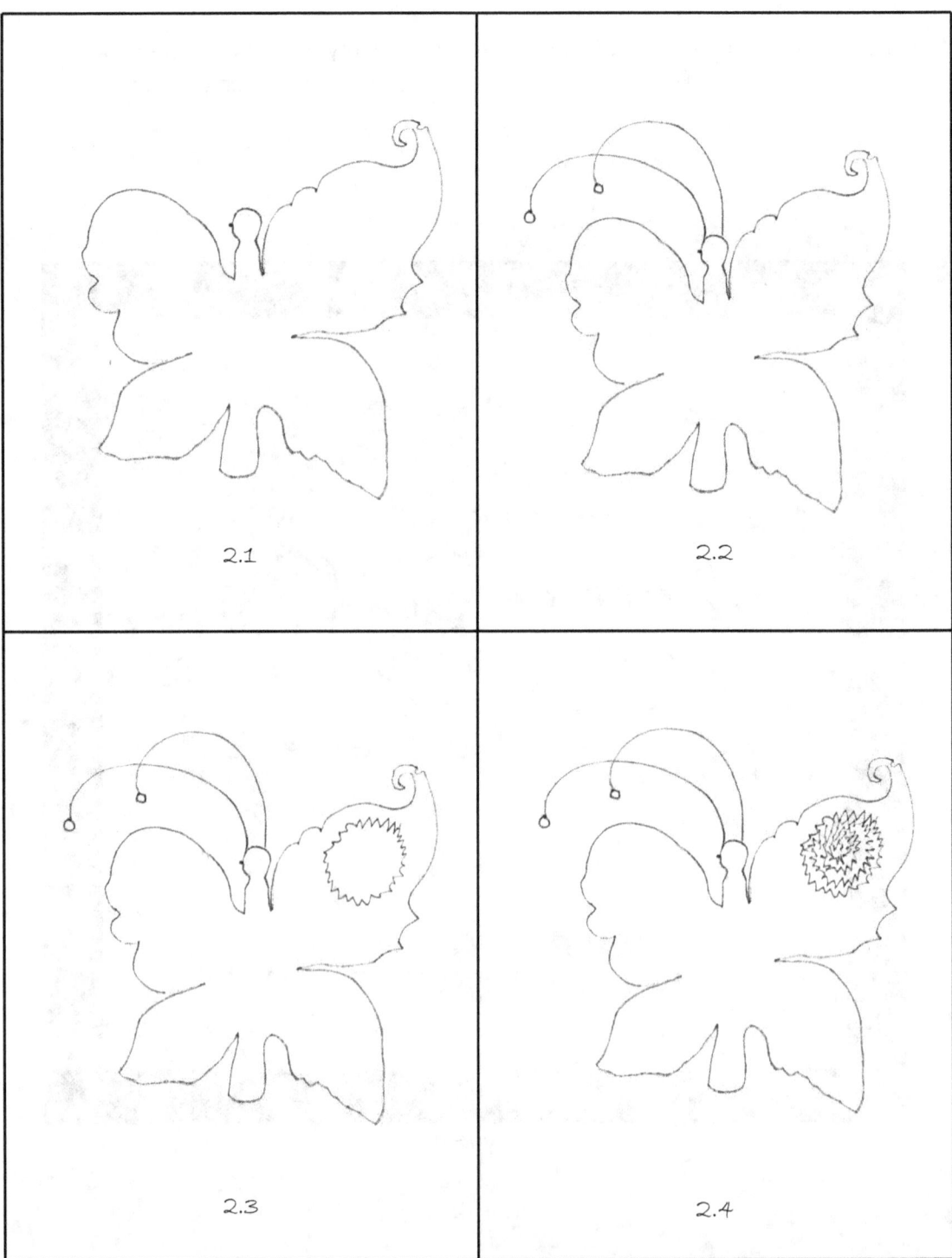

2.1

2.2

2.3

2.4

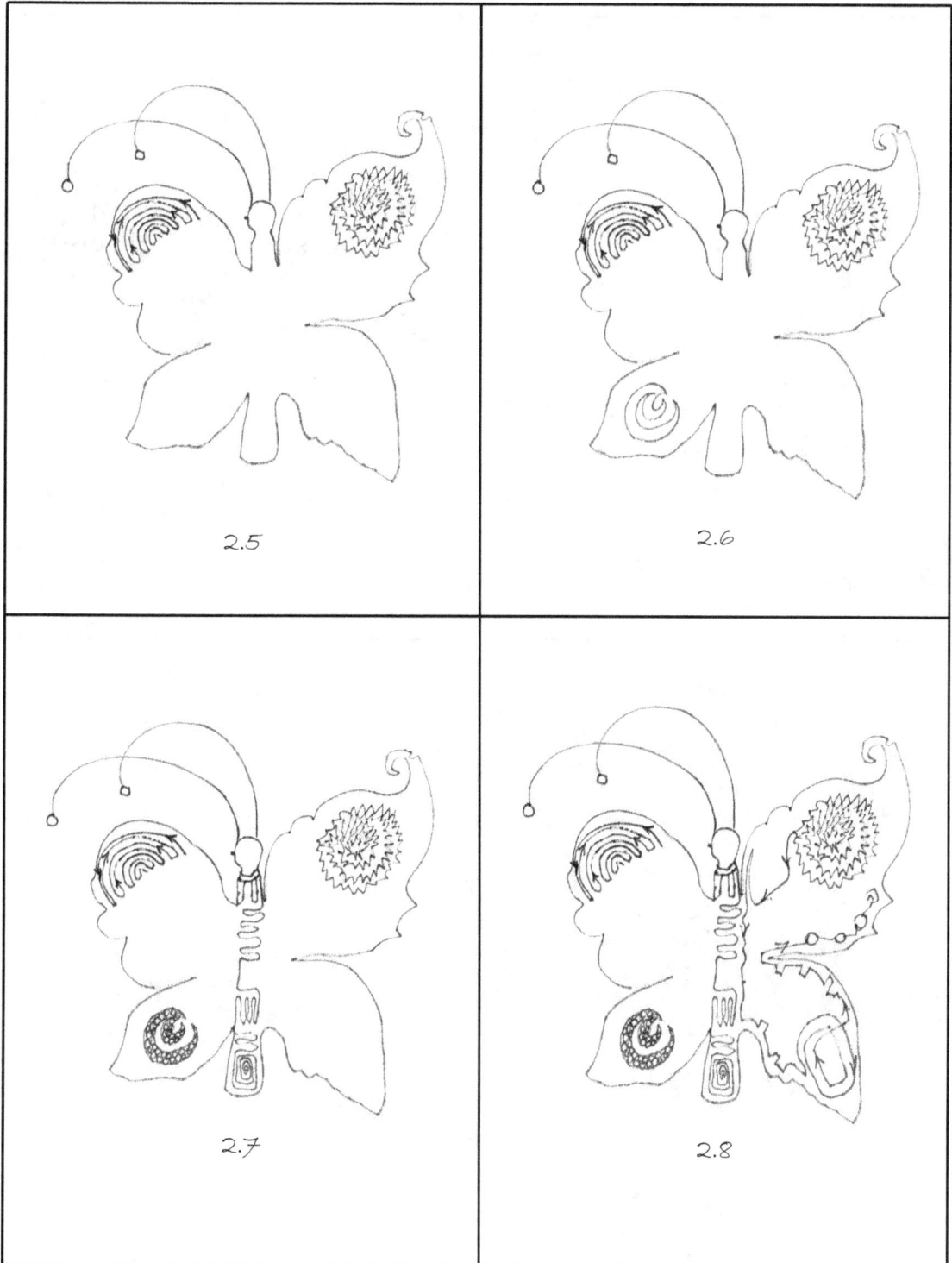

2.5

2.6

2.7

2.8

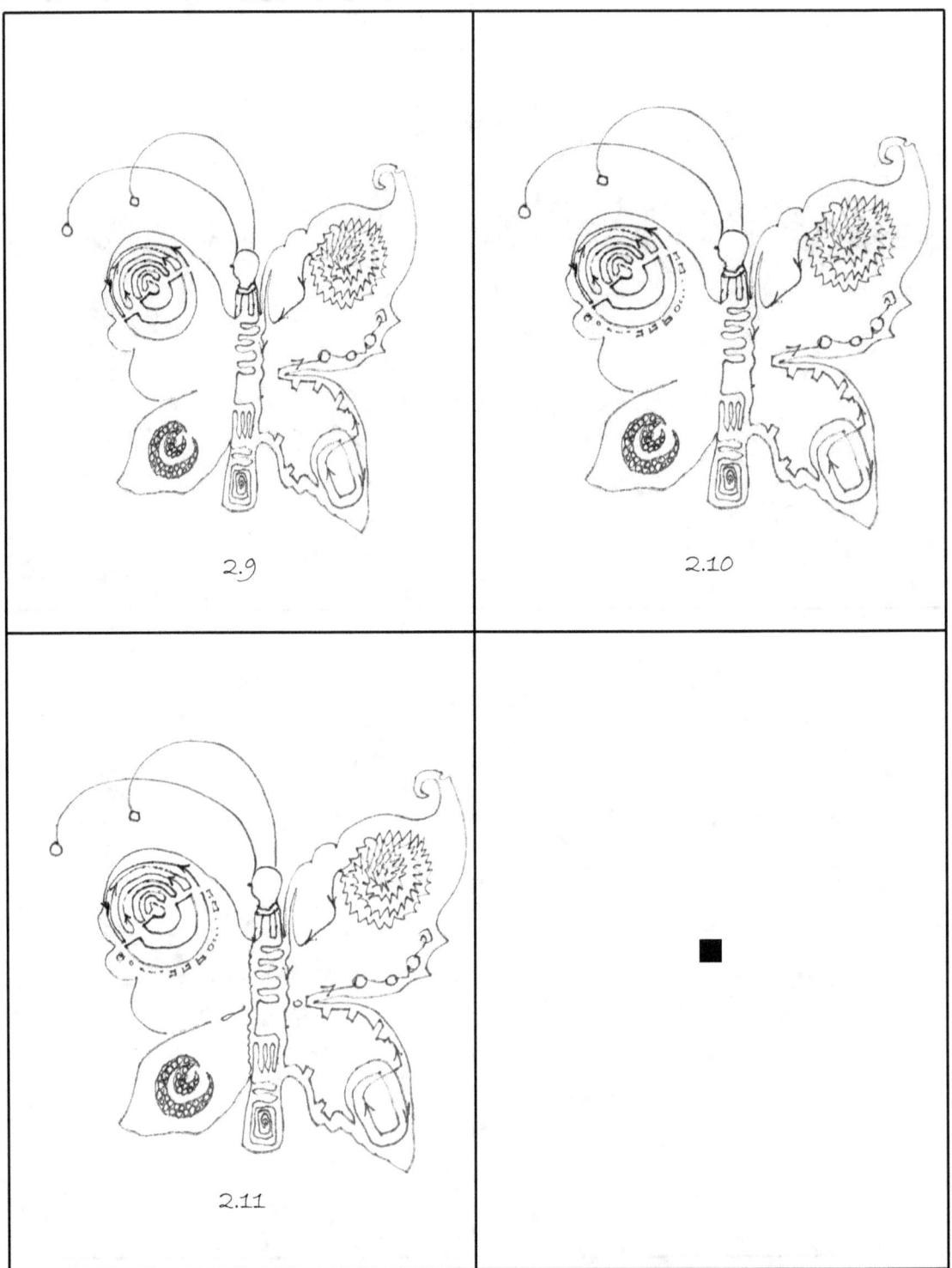

2.9

2.10

2.11

How to Draw Butterfly 3

Next pages will show you how to create NeoWhimsy Butterfly 3. The butterflies you see in this book are unique and imaginative. Imagination is a world where images are nested in the mind to form a concept of what is not actually present to the senses. You already understand the process of image developing and soon you will be able to create NeoWhimsies independently, using your imagination and artistic skills.

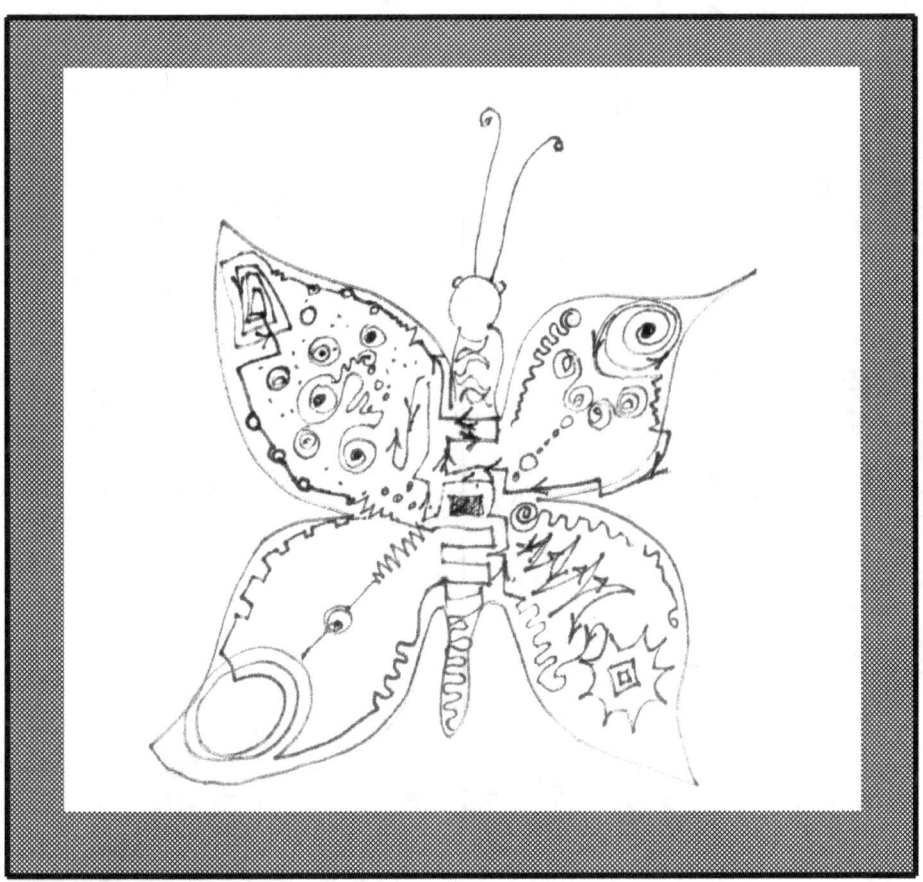

The Butterfly 3

This page includes the patterns, used in Whimsy Butterfly 3.

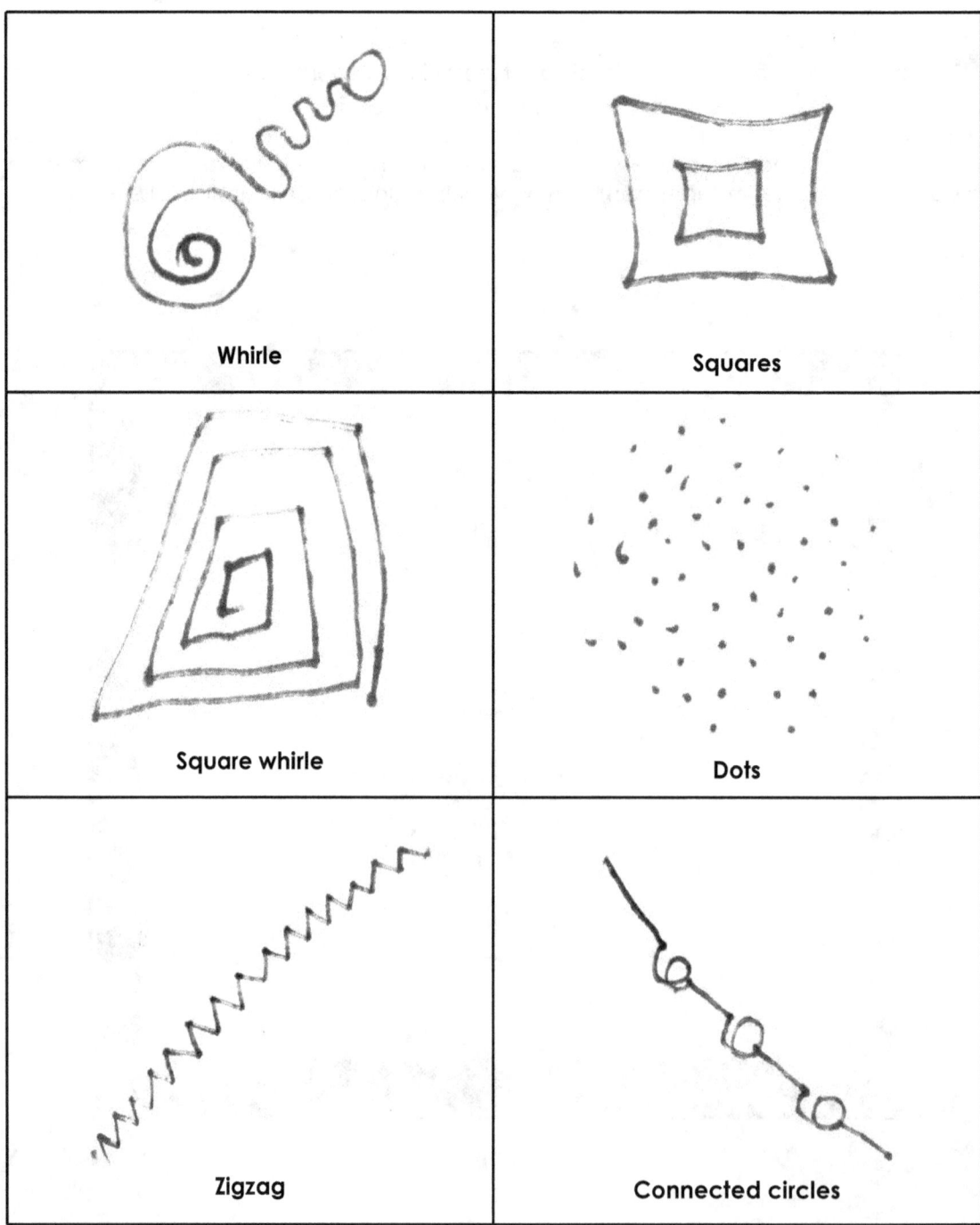

Whirle

Squares

Square whirle

Dots

Zigzag

Connected circles

The following visual instruction will show you how to draw NeoWhimsy Butterfly 3. Art is a combination of craft and imagination, skills, and inventiveness. Practice and you will be able to develop all these qualities.

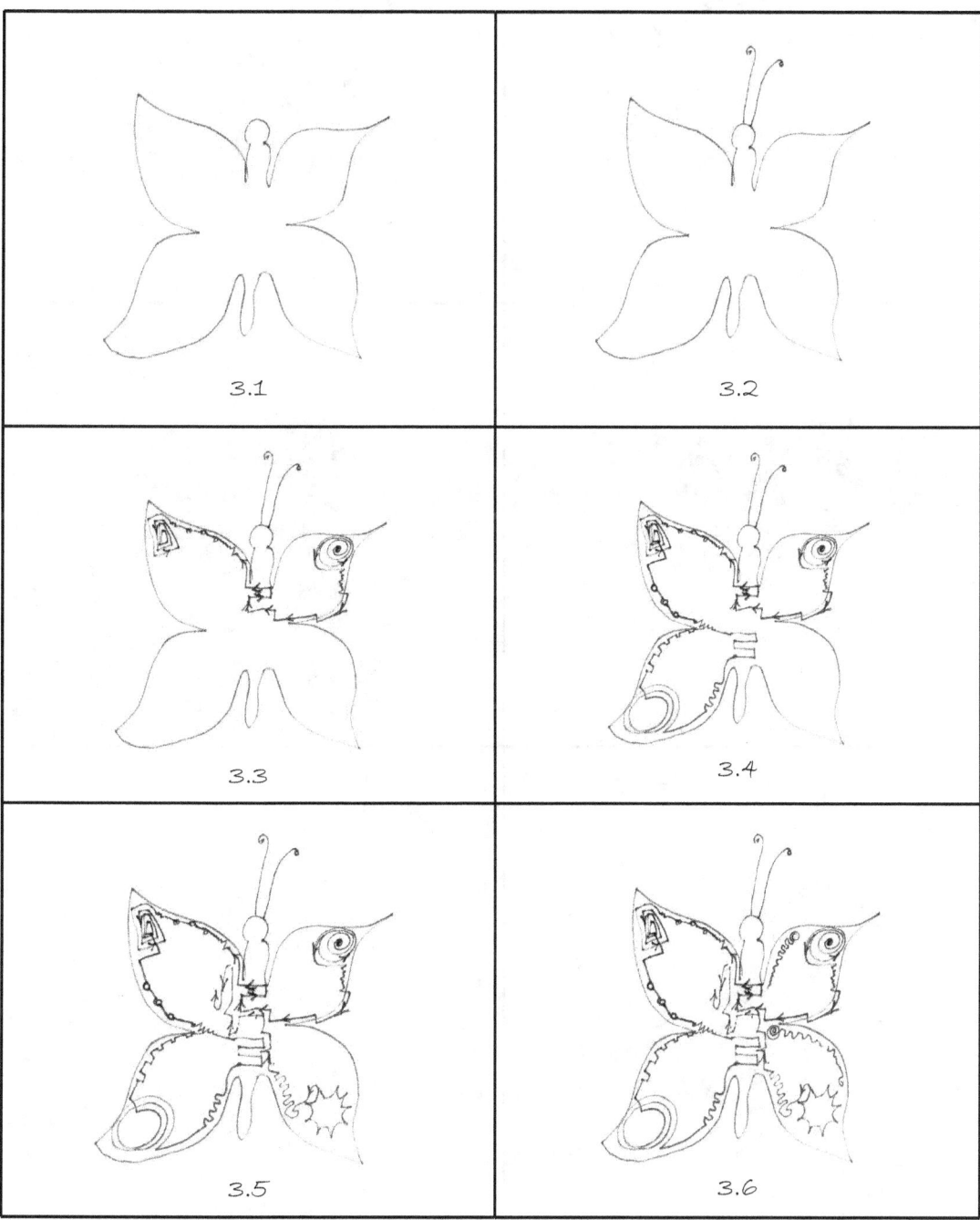

3.1

3.2

3.3

3.4

3.5

3.6

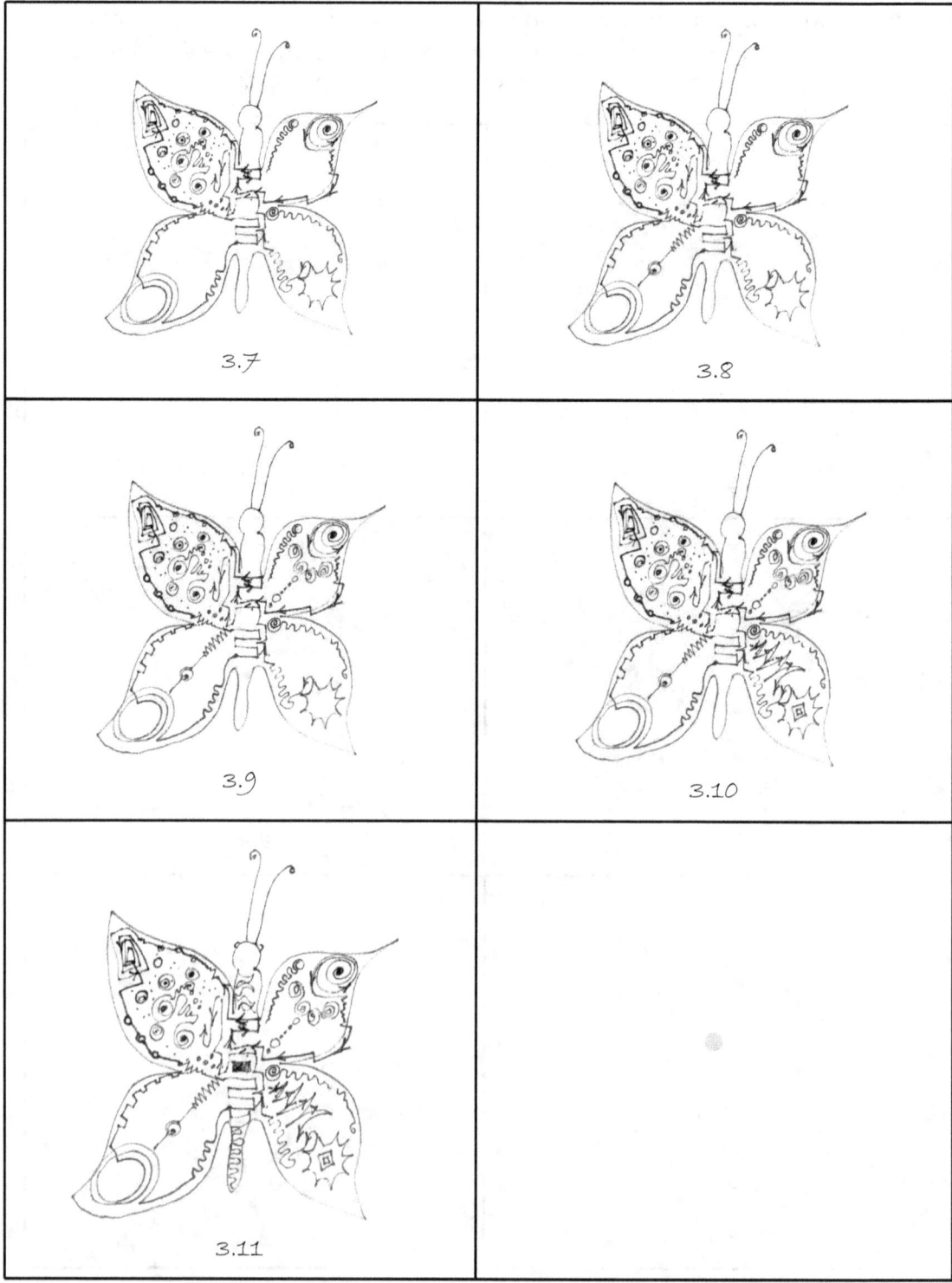

3.7

3.8

3.9

3.10

3.11

Draw the Butterflies Here and Now

Use next pages for your training. Get your ink pen and fill the sections of images of butterflies with different patterns. Let your imagination lead you, create new patterns, follow your creative senses. Some section(s) leave blank. Nothing is impossible. When you draw the repetitive patterns you enter meditative state of mind, your brain is relaxing. This drawing helps you to achieve both the interesting artistic results and purity of your mind. More you practice, better your NeoWhimsies are.

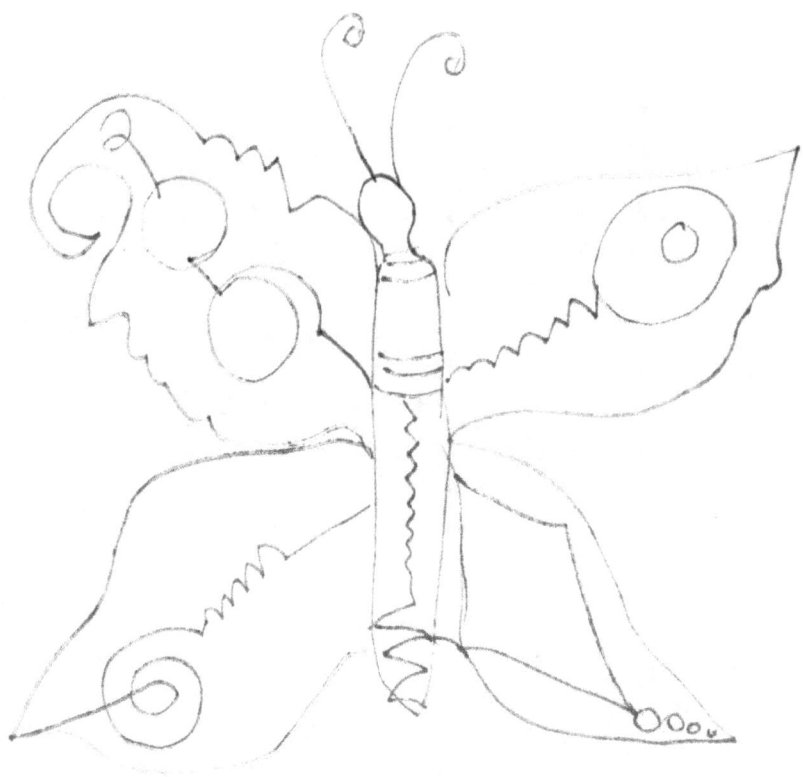

The Butterfly 1

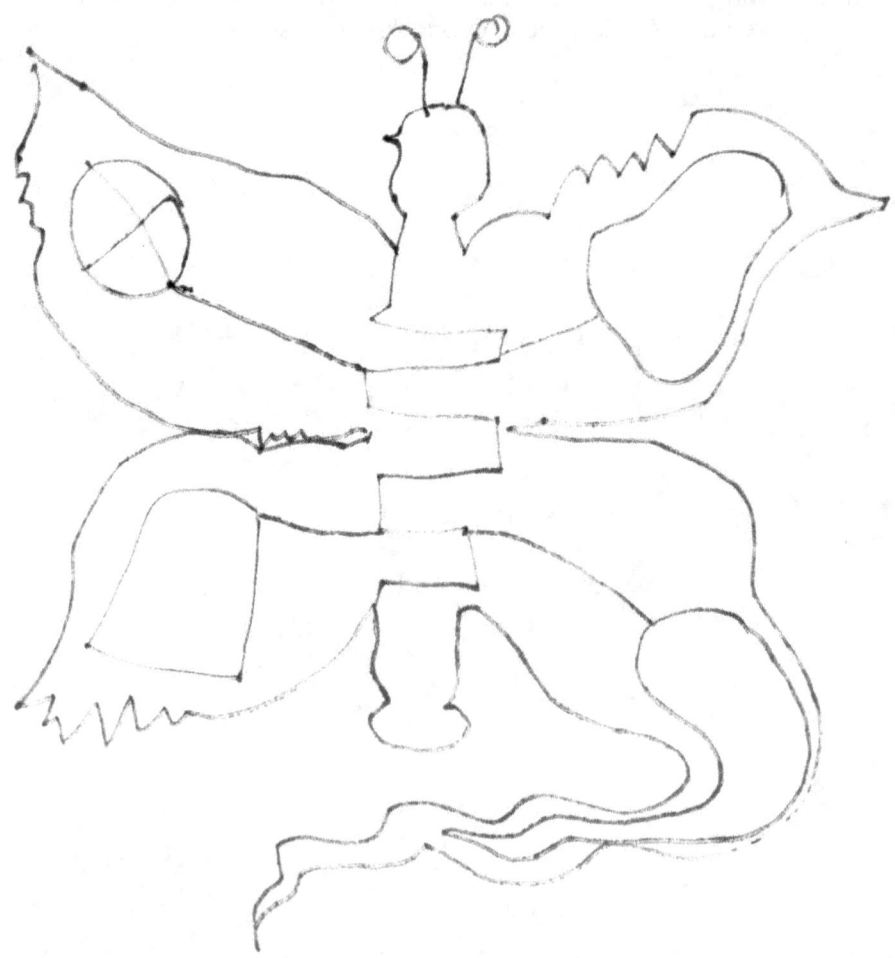

The Butterfly 2

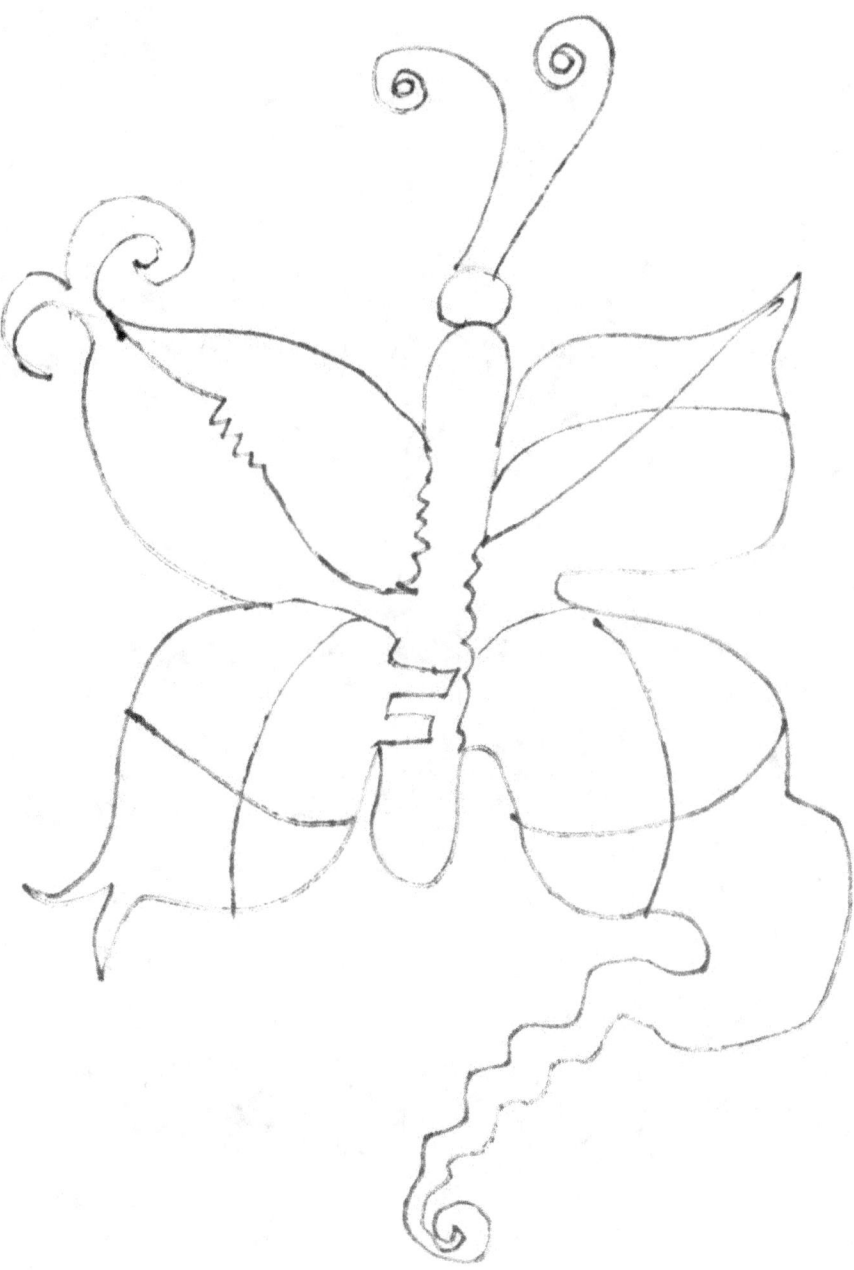

The Butterfly 3

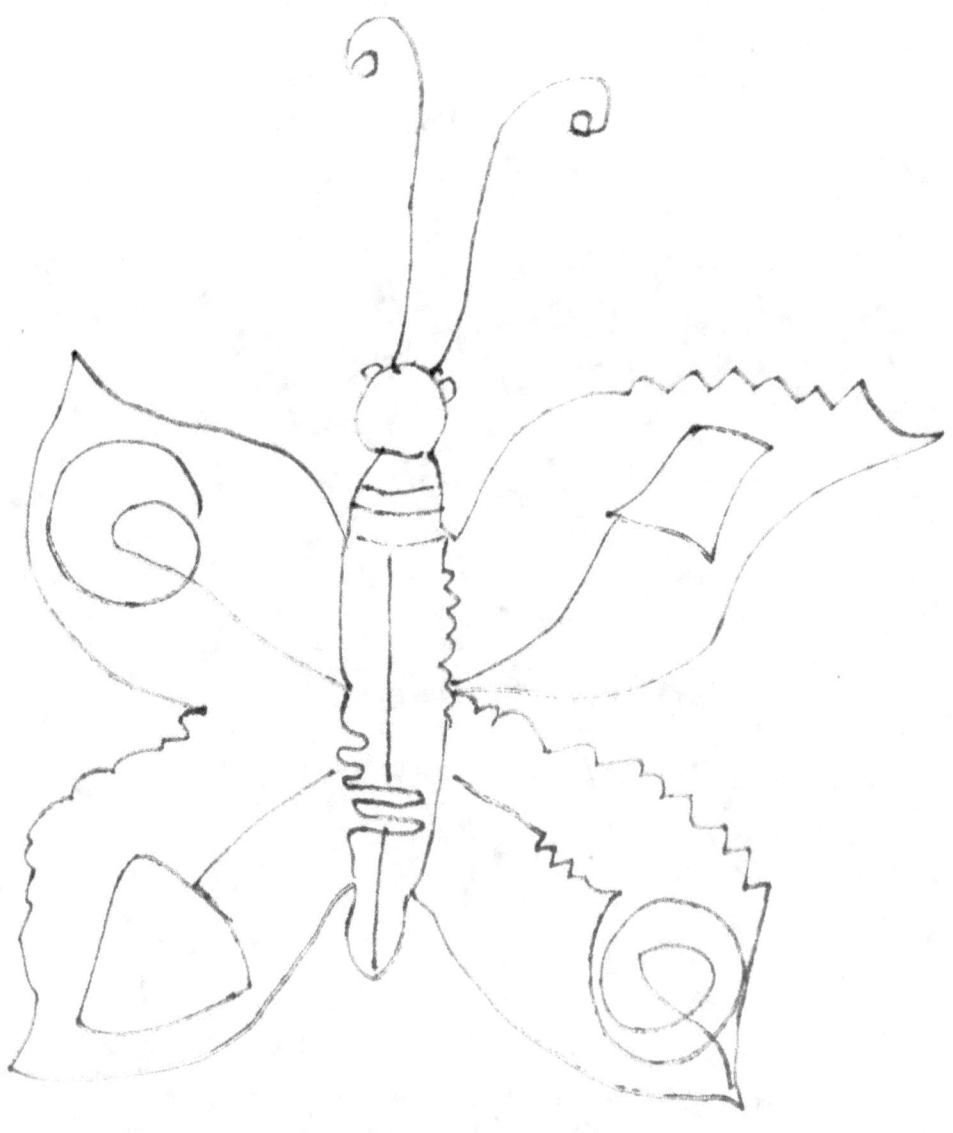

The Butterfly 4

NeoWhimsies: NeoPopRealism Ink Drawing Basics for Mannequins

Draw the Flowers

T he following pages will teach you how to create NeoWhimsies Flowers. Your drawing is a reflection of your thoughts. Through the line and patterns - ornaments - you are sharing your feelings, emotions and your imagination. The practicing helps you to overcome the limitations, which stand in the way of achieving the result you want. Success is not about focusing just on your strengths, it is more about stretching yourself beyond your limits. The drawing will help you learn more about yourself. Focus on self-improvement, think of limitation you have as the challenges, not weaknesses. Have passion and confidence and your attitude will change everything.

The following visual instructions will lead you from the beginning to end of the entire drawing process. Every following image includes new detail(s). The final images look like this:

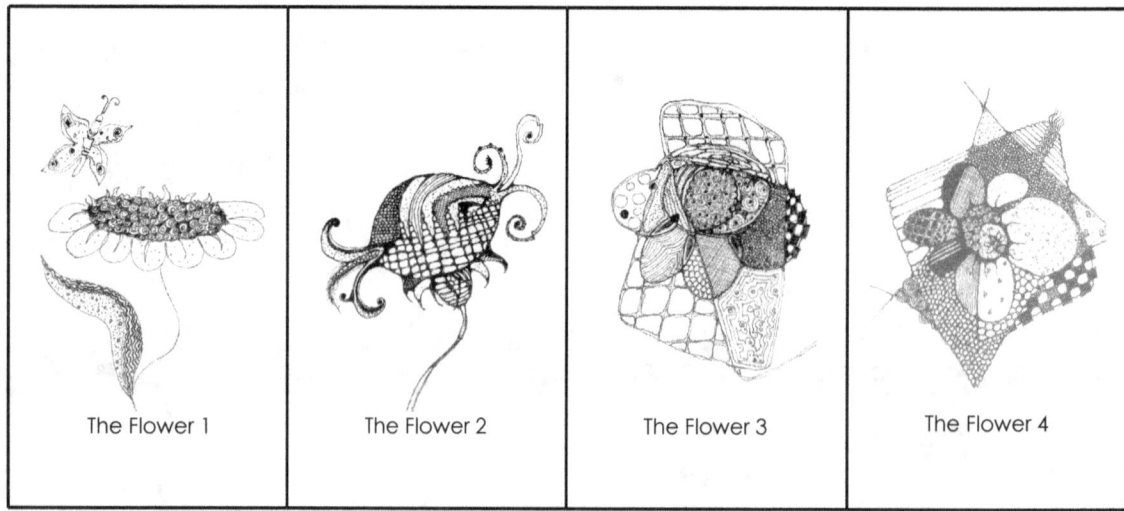

| The Flower 1 | The Flower 2 | The Flower 3 | The Flower 4 |

How to Draw Flower 1

This page includes the patterns used in NeoWhimsy Flower 1.

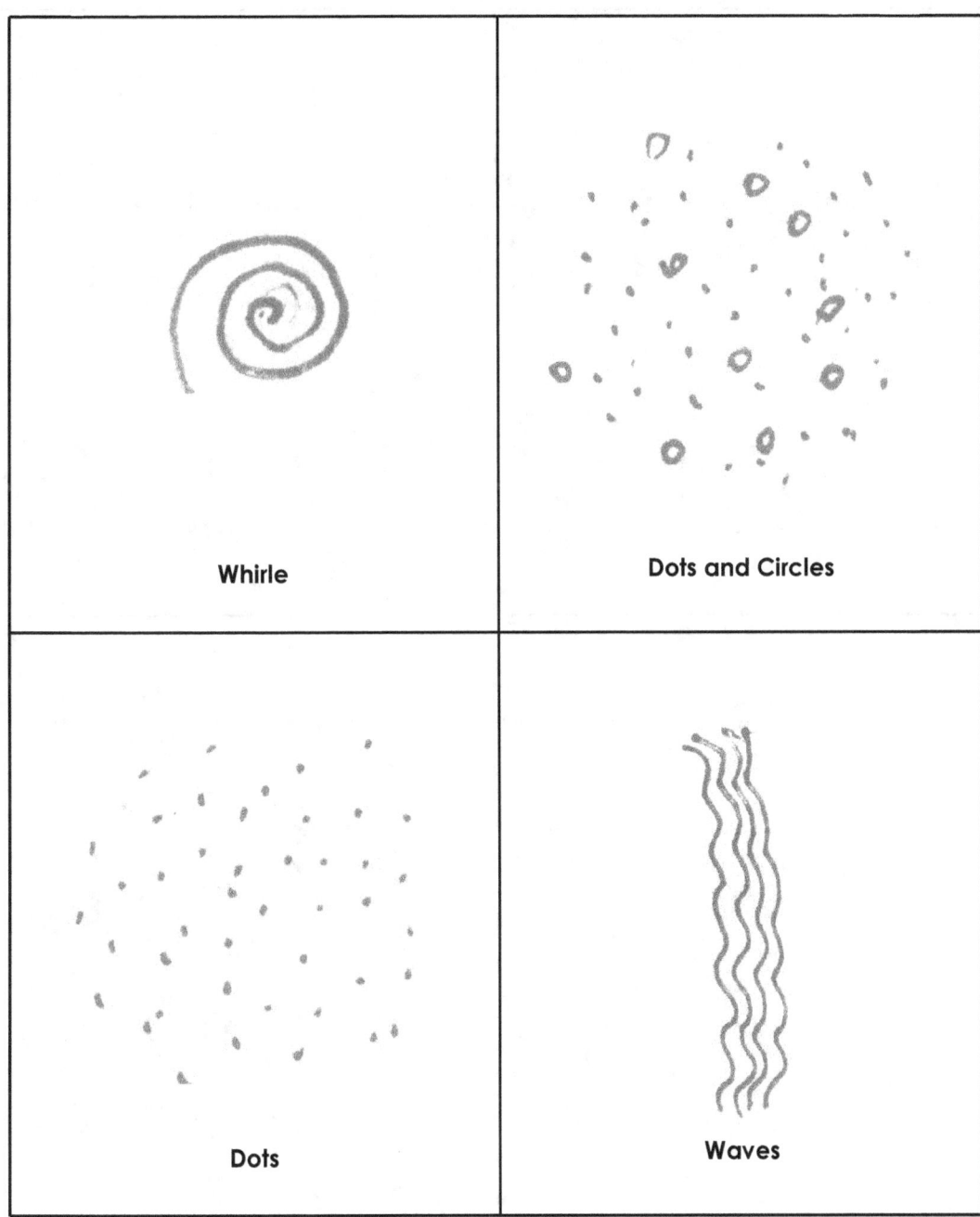

Whirle

Dots and Circles

Dots

Waves

The drawings are like music, they can be happy, sad, mysterious, simple, and complicated. They reflect the artist's vision and feelings. . .

The following visual instructions will show you step-by-step how to draw NeoWhimsy Flower 1.

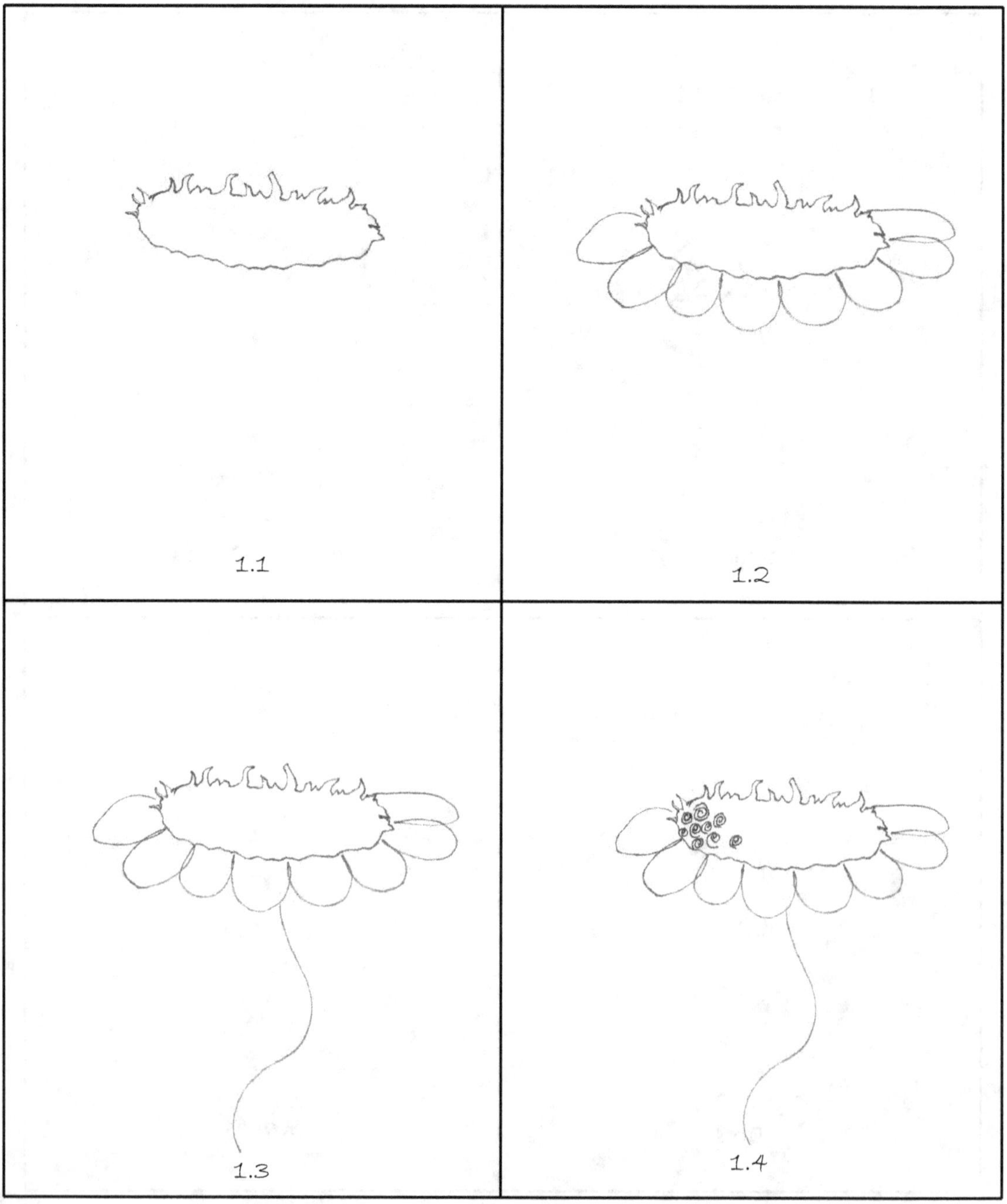

1.1

1.2

1.3

1.4

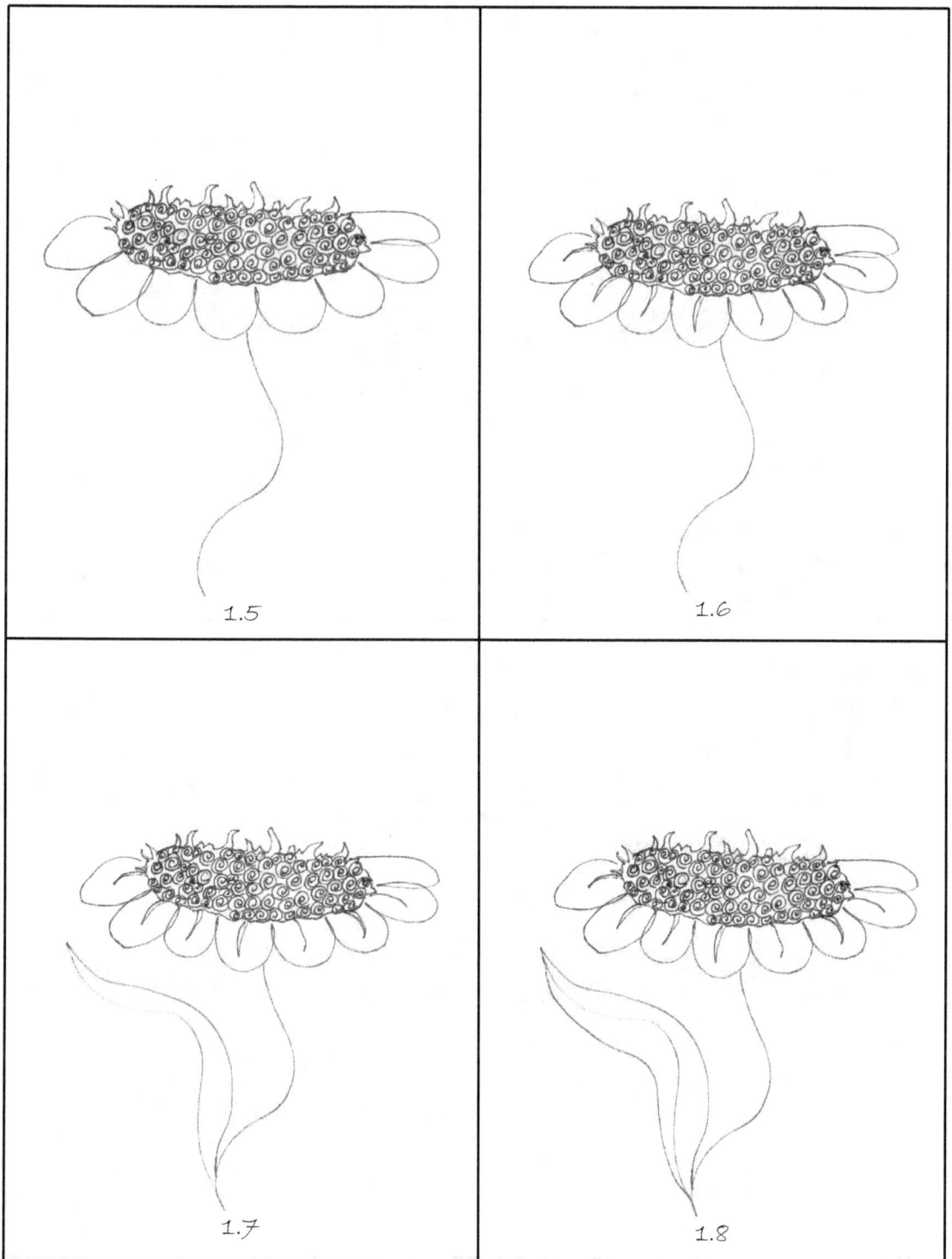

1.5

1.6

1.7

1.8

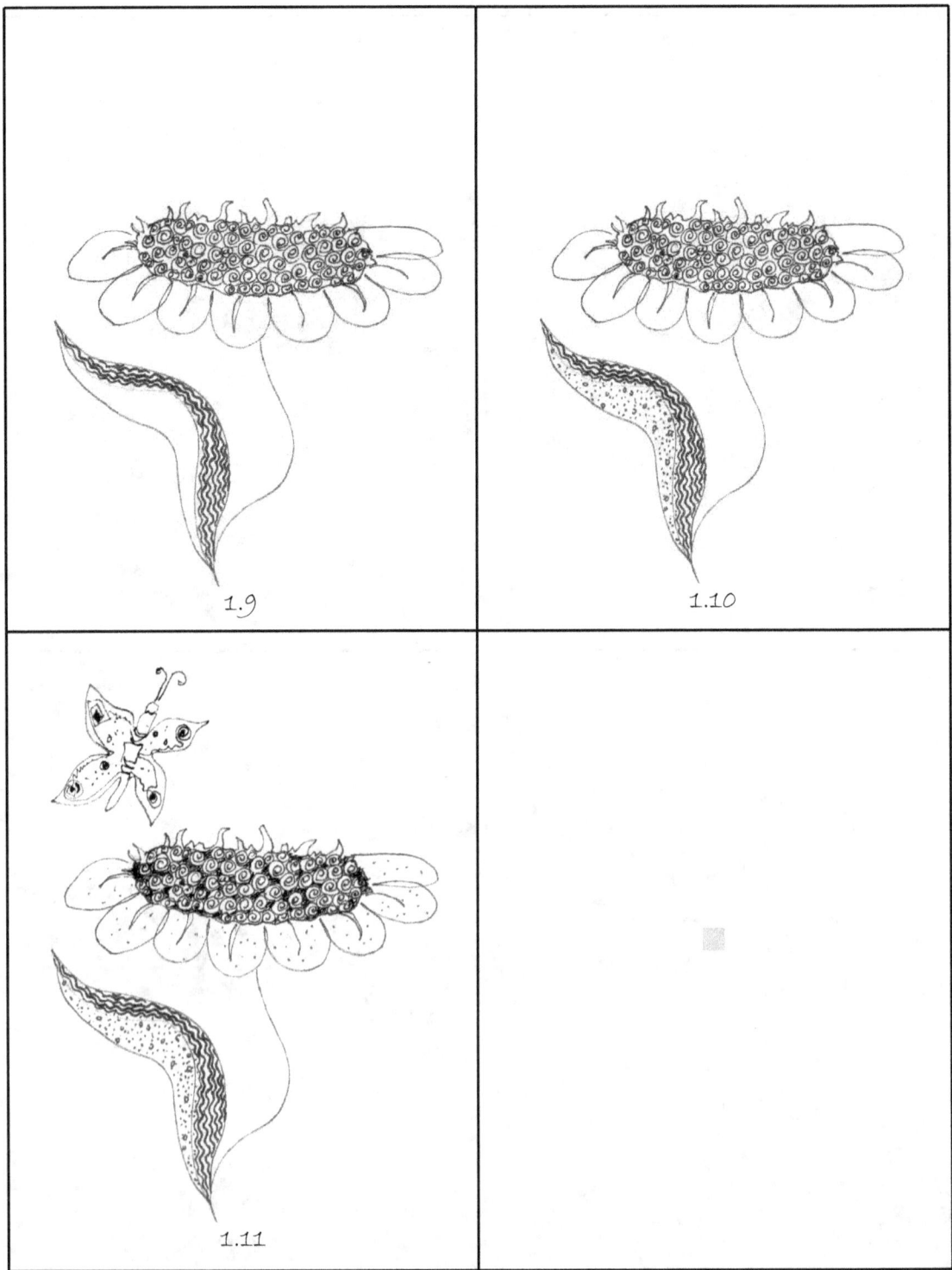

1.9

1.10

1.11

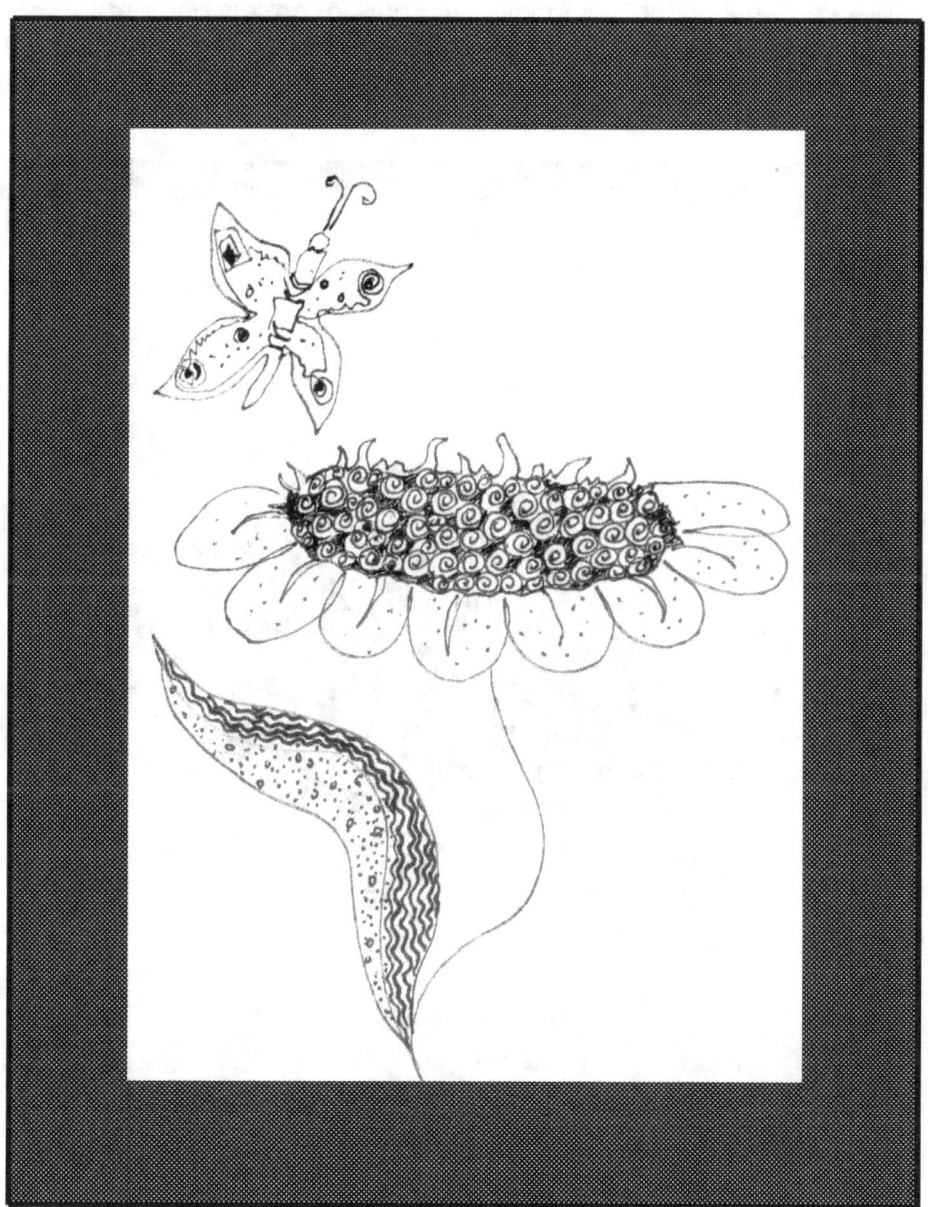

The Flower 1

How to Draw Flower 2

Our world is challenging and demanding. It produces anxiety and stress. Everything is transforming every minute and is waiting for you to get on board. Open your mind and explore what is possible, employing your talent and skills. Learn, create, meditate!

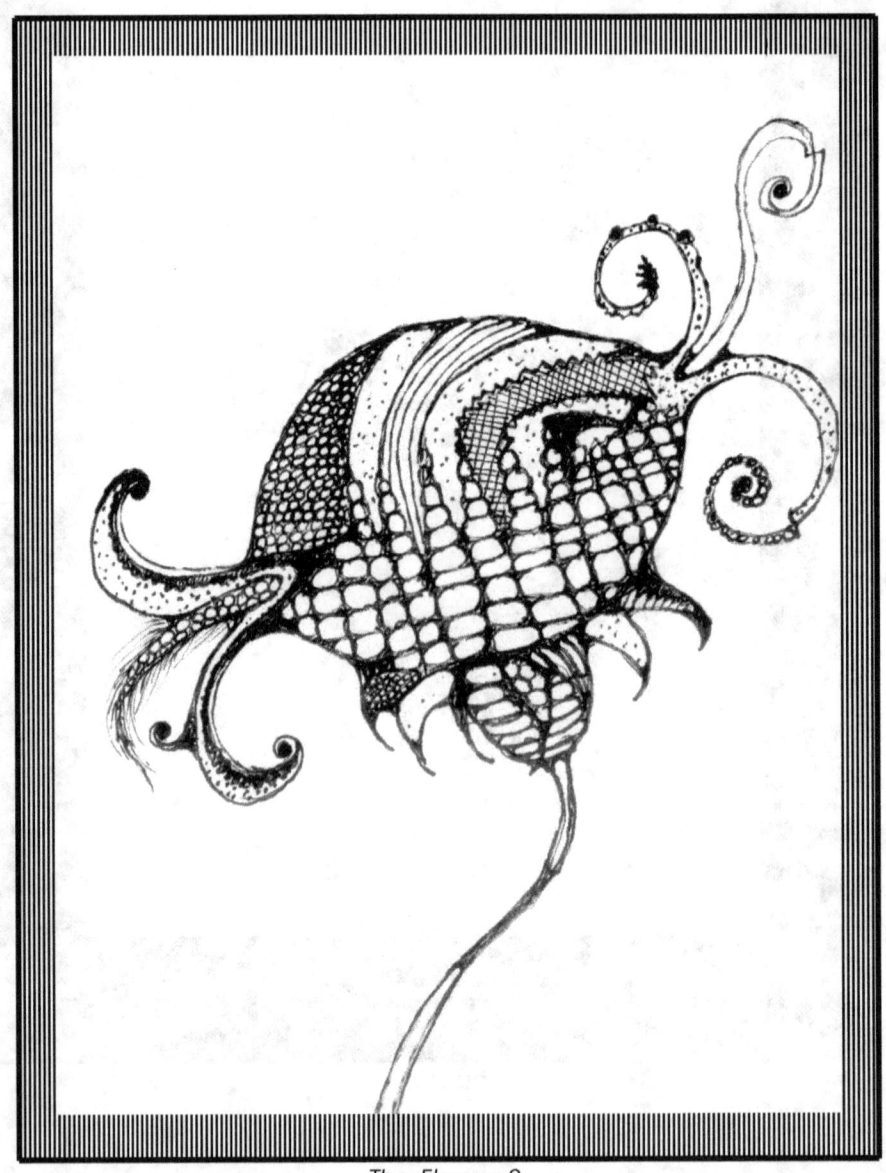

The Flower 2

Explore patterns, used in The Flower 2.

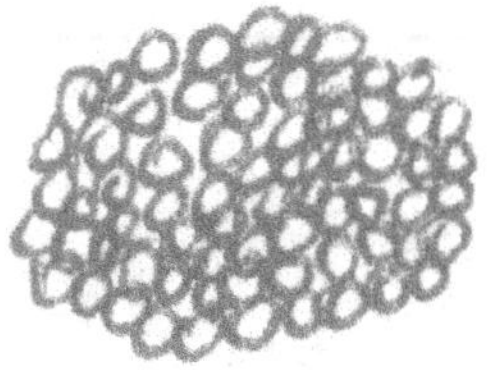

Caviar

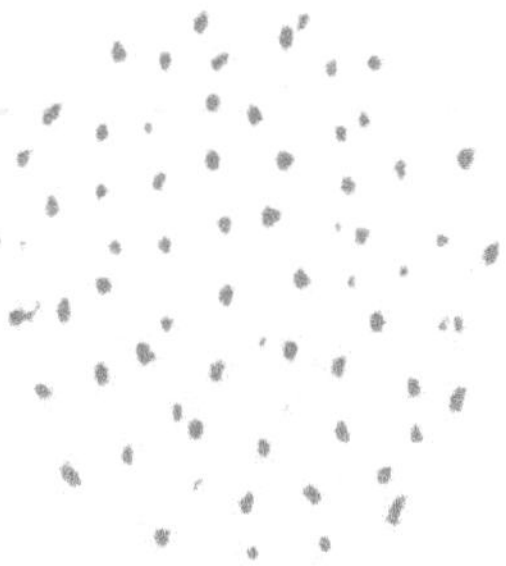

Dots

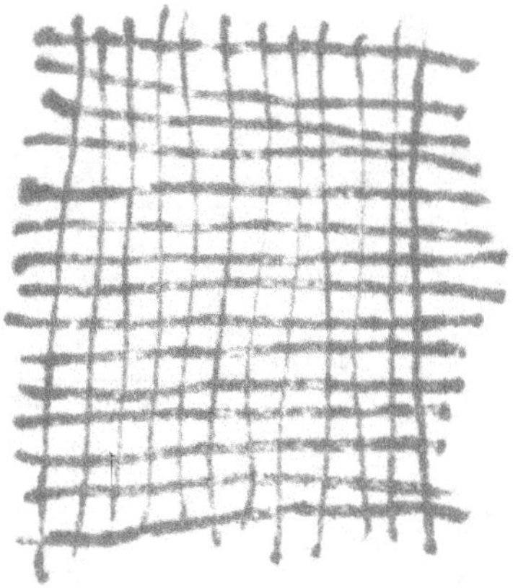

Squares

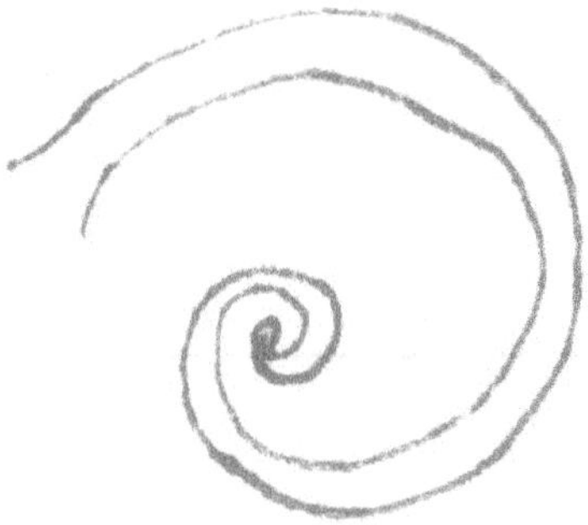

Whirle

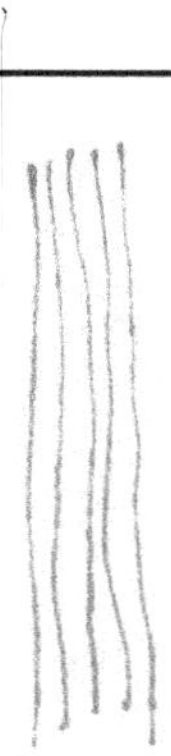

Strips

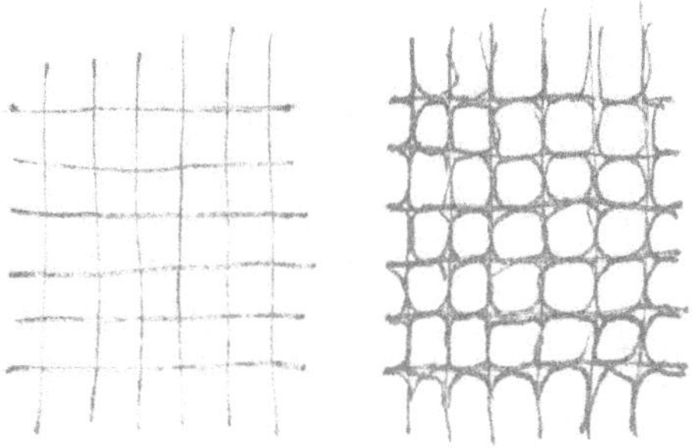

Squares with softened angles

Next pages will teach you how to draw The Flower 2. Step-by-step you will follow the visual instructions. Practice and you will draw your NeoWhimsies with ease, your line will flow smooth and the compositions of your artworks will be more and more interesting and imaginative.

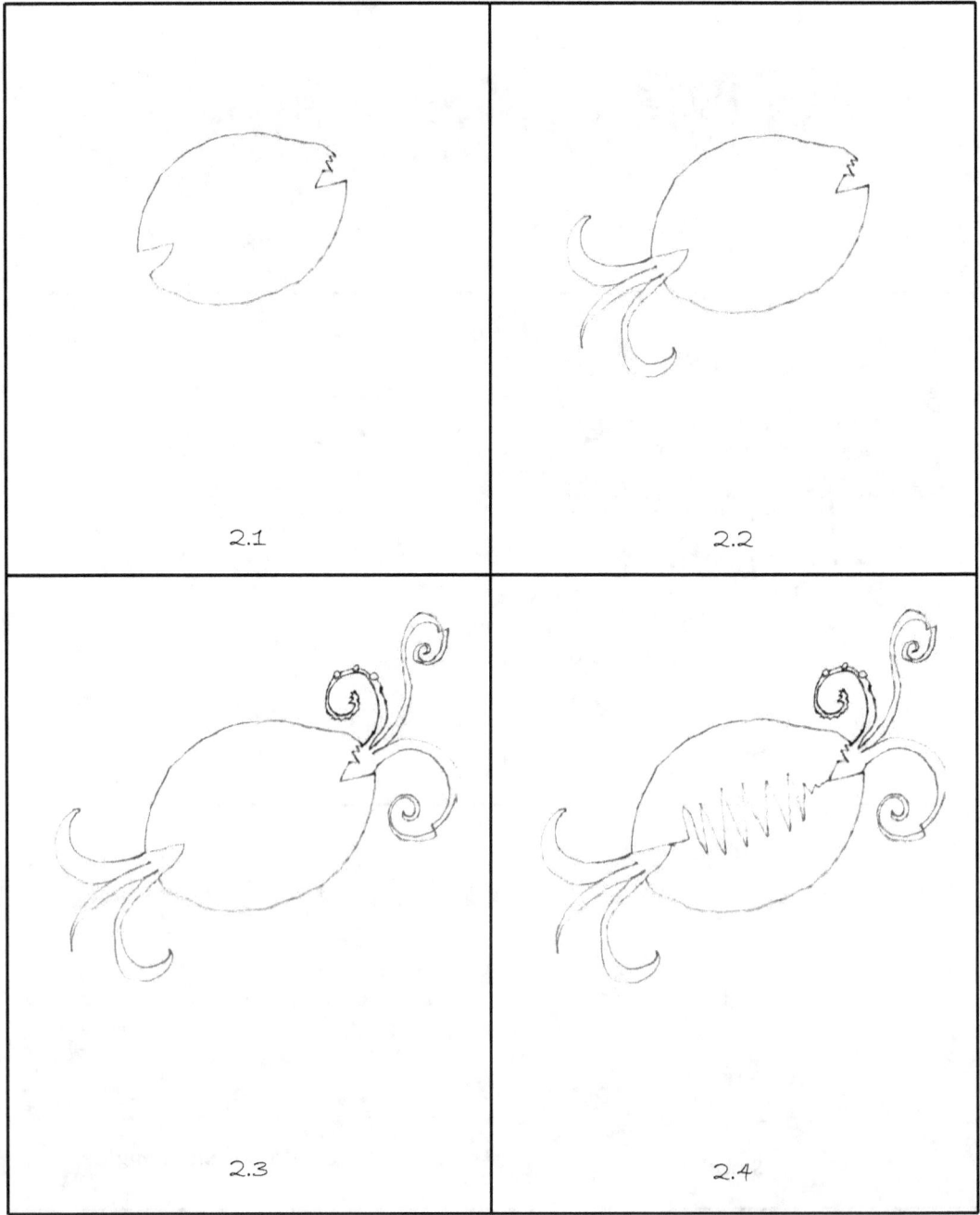

2.1

2.2

2.3

2.4

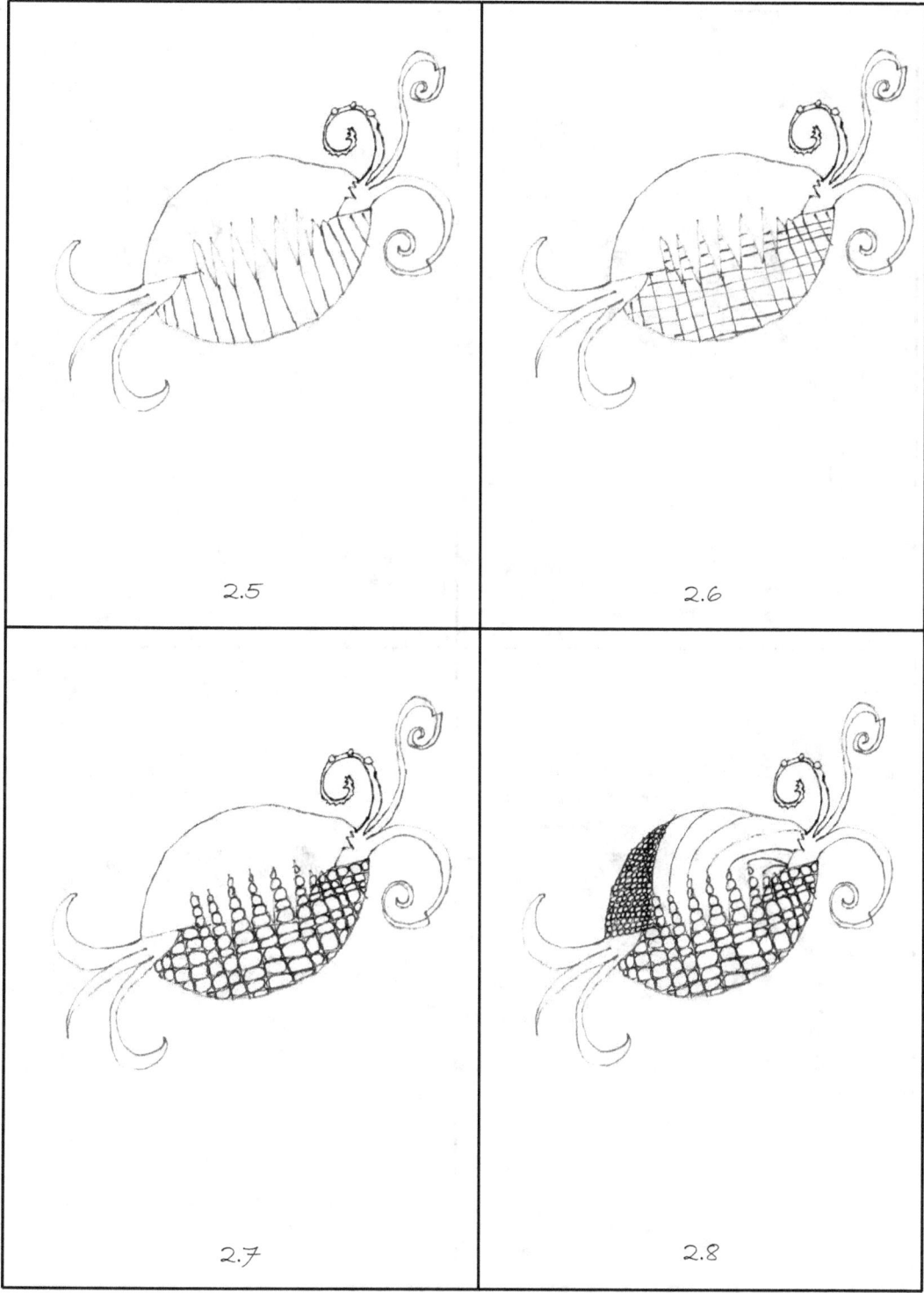

2.5

2.6

2.7

2.8

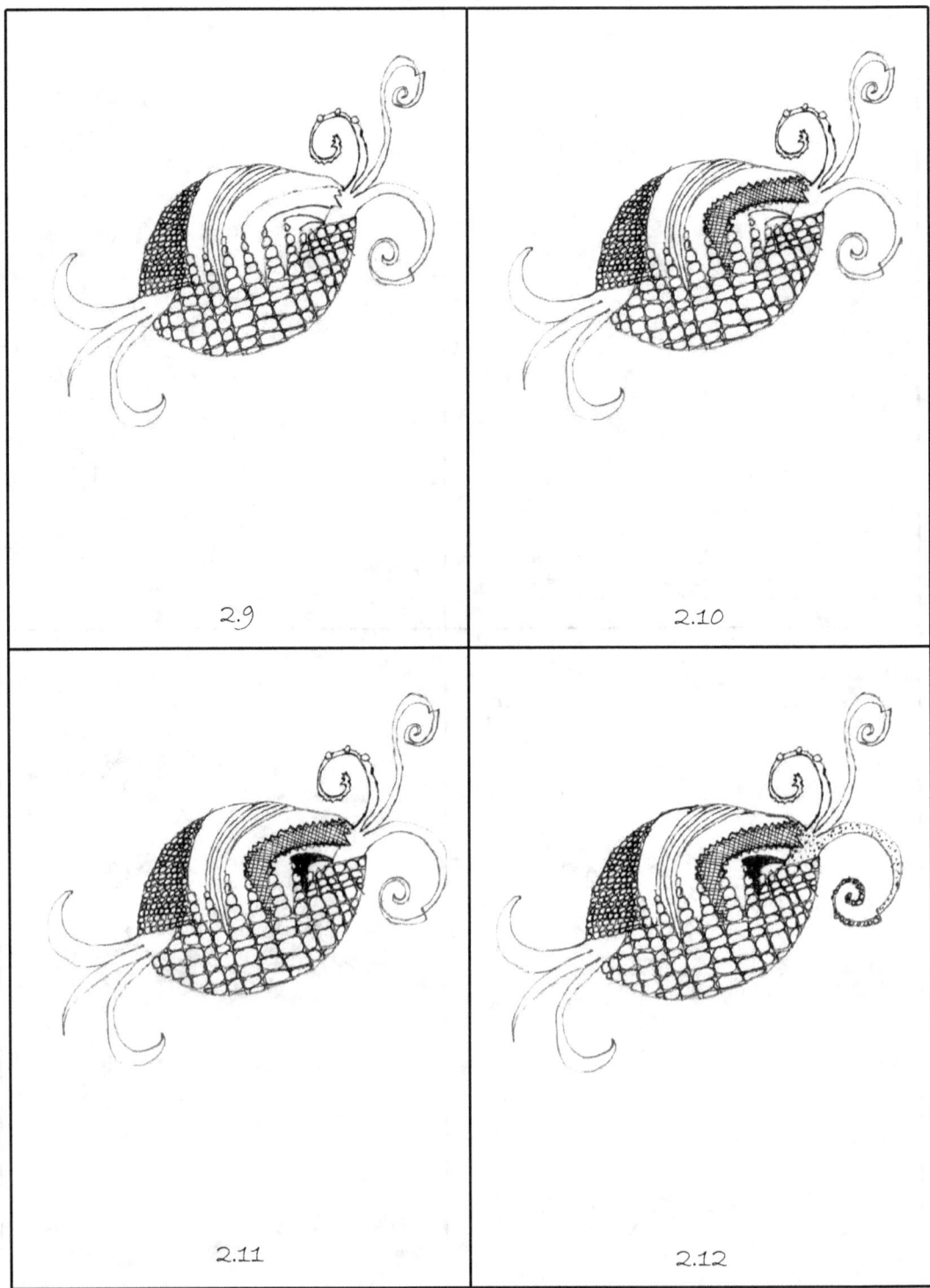

2.9

2.10

2.11

2.12

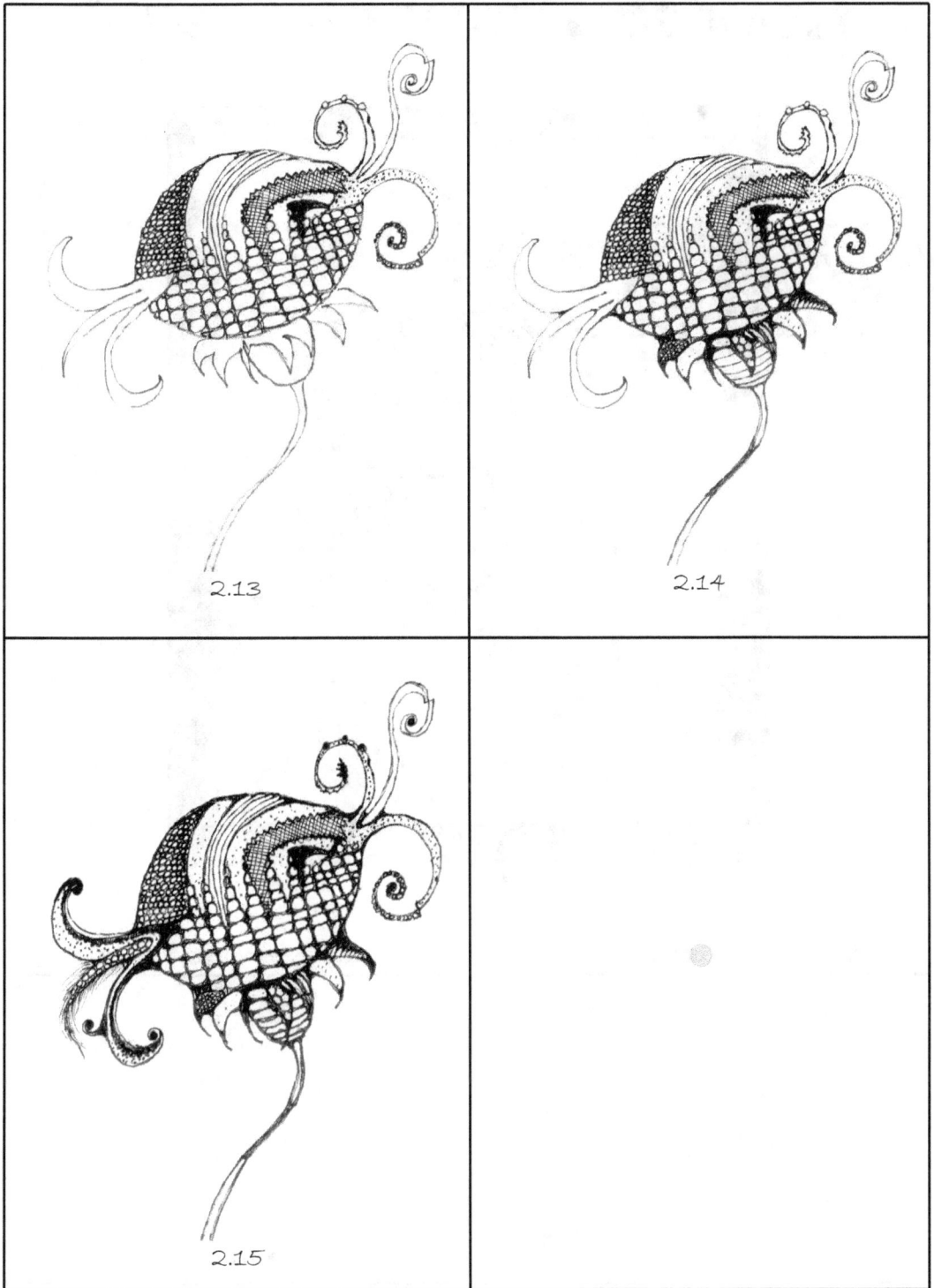

2.13

2.14

2.15

How to Draw Flower 3

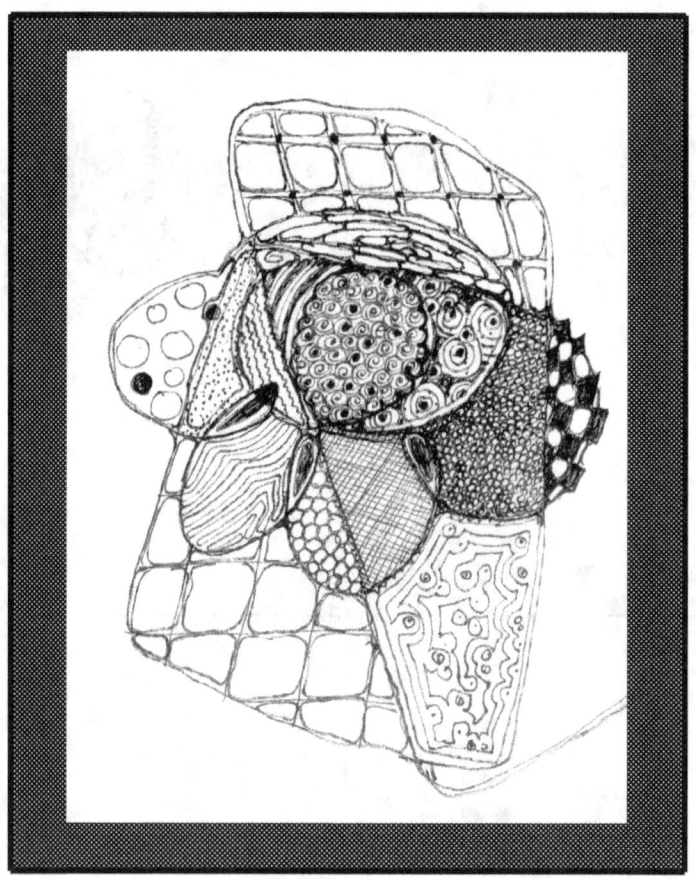

The Flower 3

Learn how to draw the repetitive patterns used in NeoWhimsy *Flower 3*.

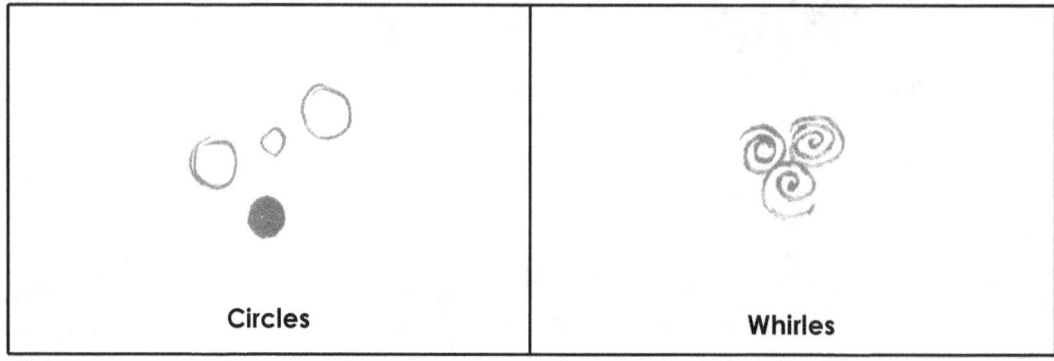

| Circles | Whirles |

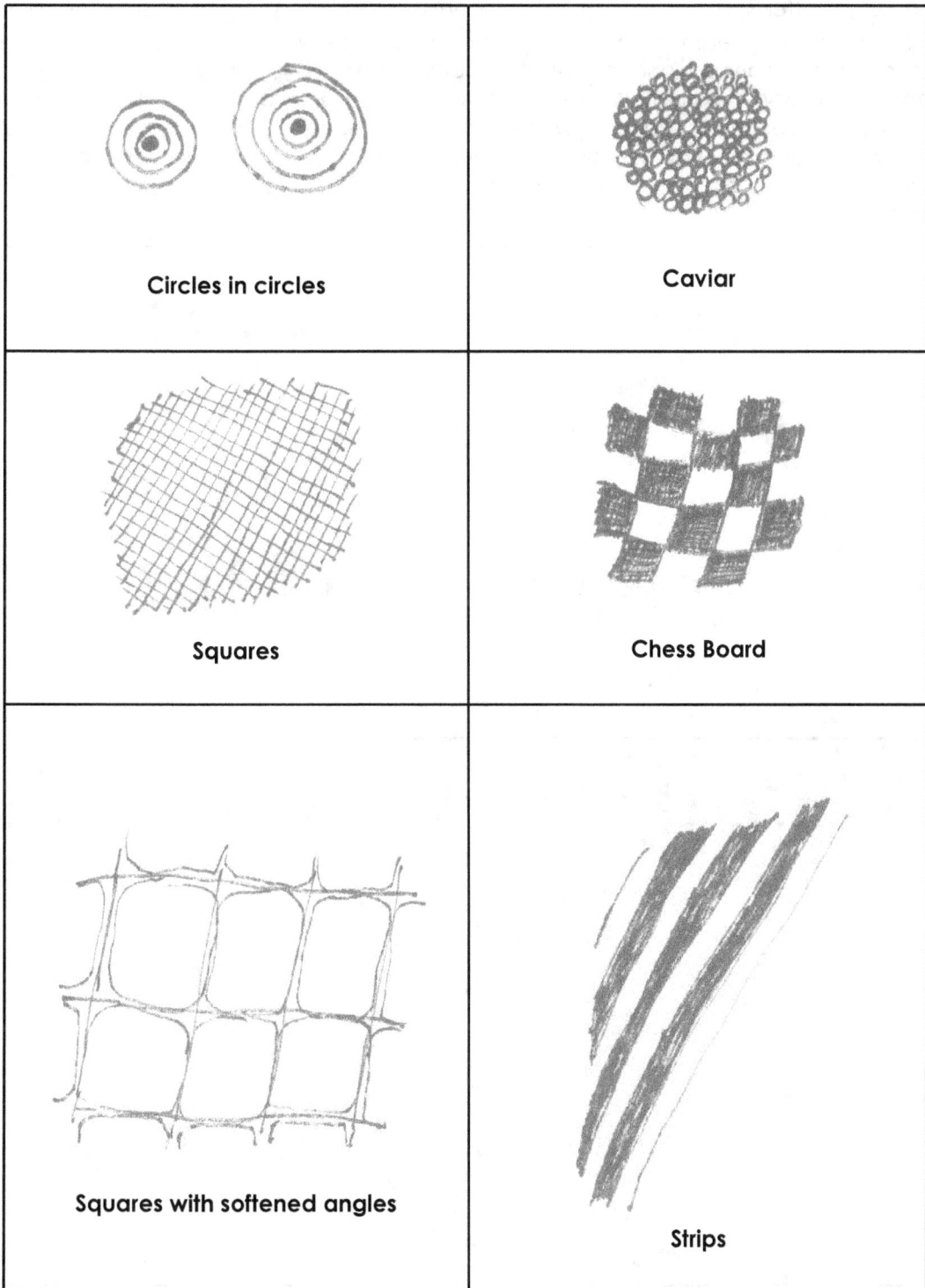

Circles in circles

Caviar

Squares

Chess Board

Squares with softened angles

Strips

Next pages offer you the visual instructions that show how to draw NeoWhimsy Flower 3. Step-by-step you will learn the developing process from beginning to end, you will learn how to create the balanced and beautiful images using your intuition and artistic skills. This composition is asymmetrical. Creation of this drawing could be compared to playing the Syncopation in Jazz. Syncopation is where the strong beat has been moved to a beat that is normally a weak beat. Practice and soon you will draw your NeoWhimsies with ease, your line will flow smooth and the compositions of your artworks will be more and more interesting and imaginative.

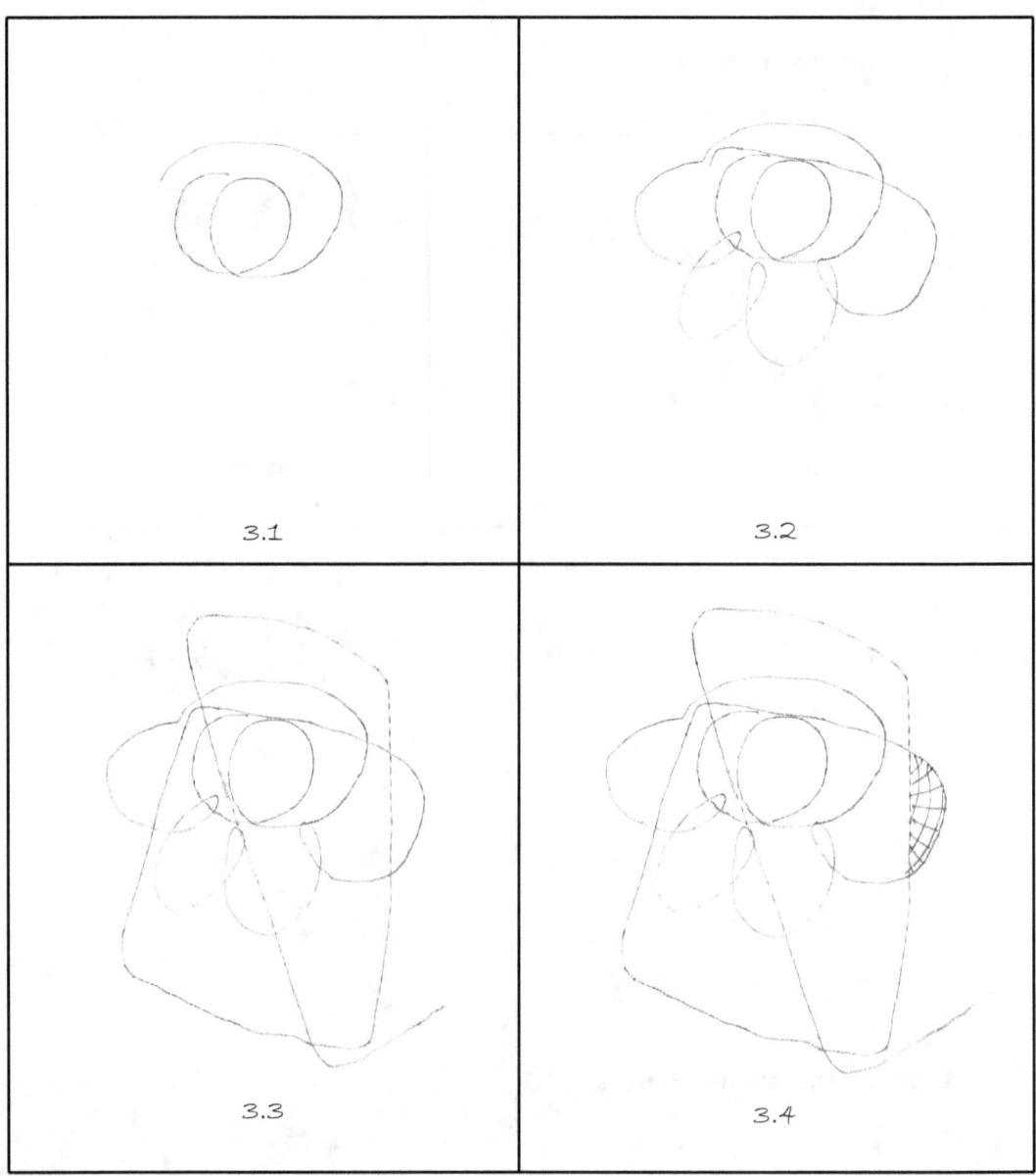

3.1

3.2

3.3

3.4

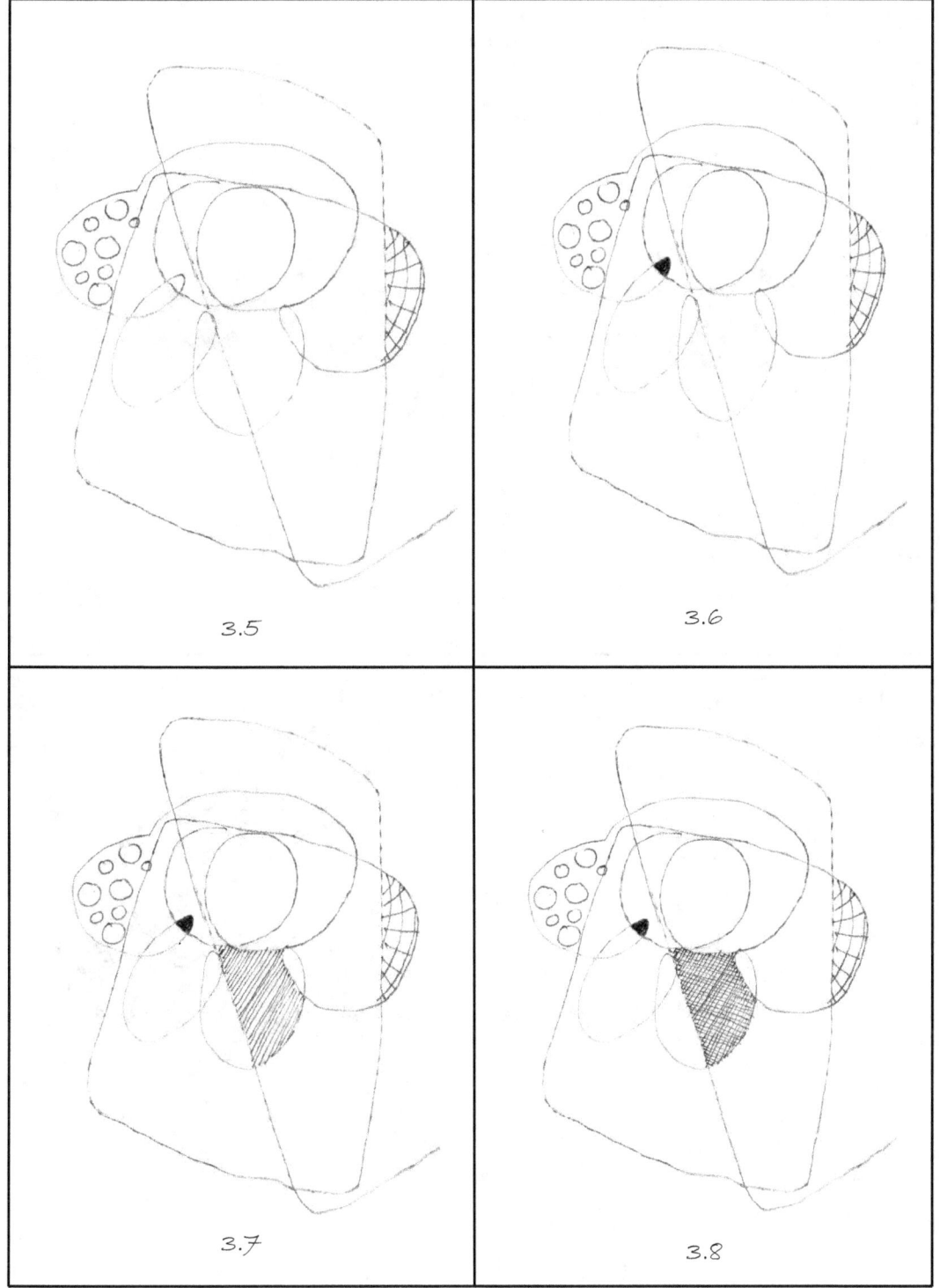

3.5

3.6

3.7

3.8

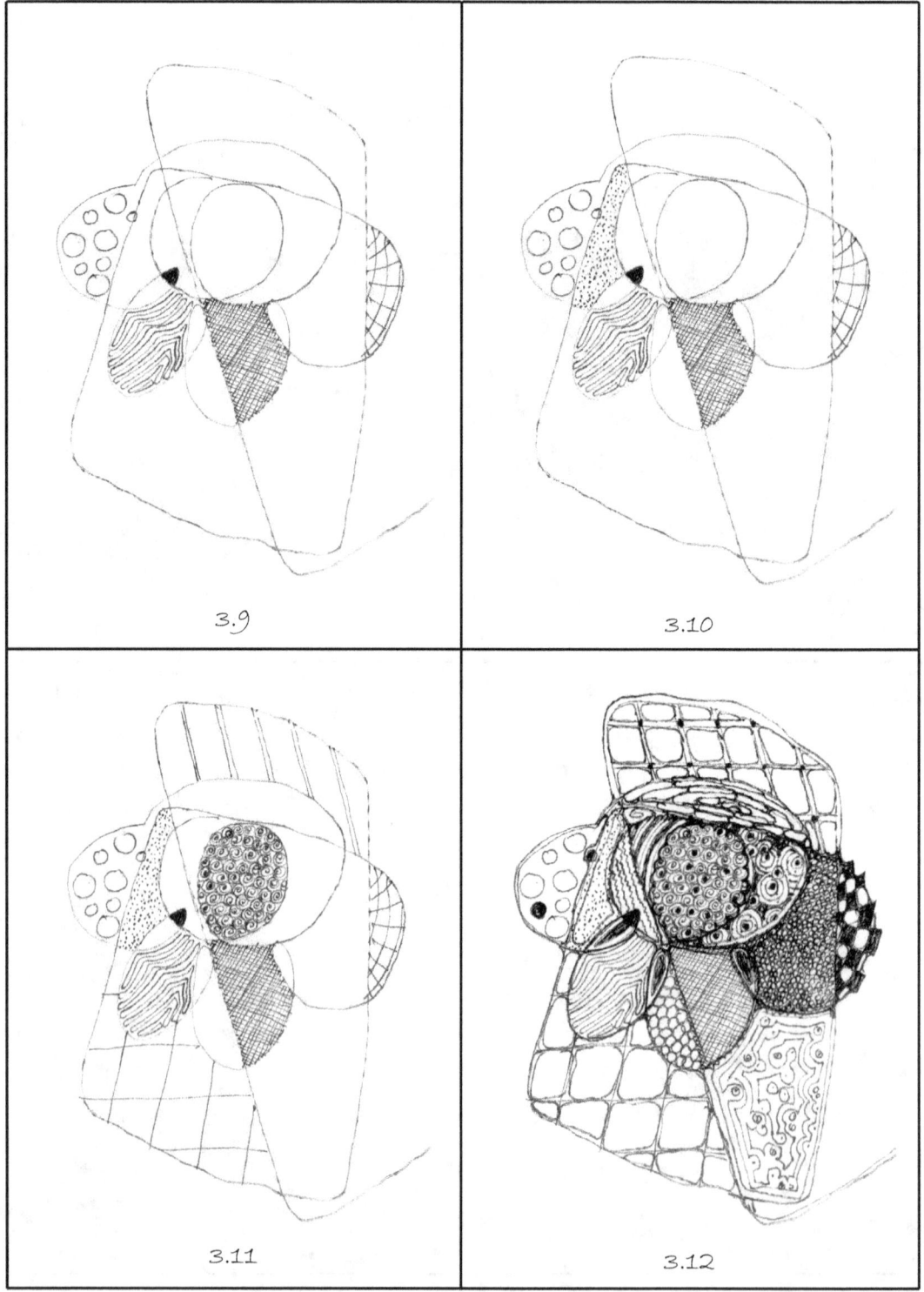

3.9

3.10

3.11

3.12

NeoWhimsies: NeoPopRealism Ink Drawing Basics for Mannequins

How to Draw Flower 4

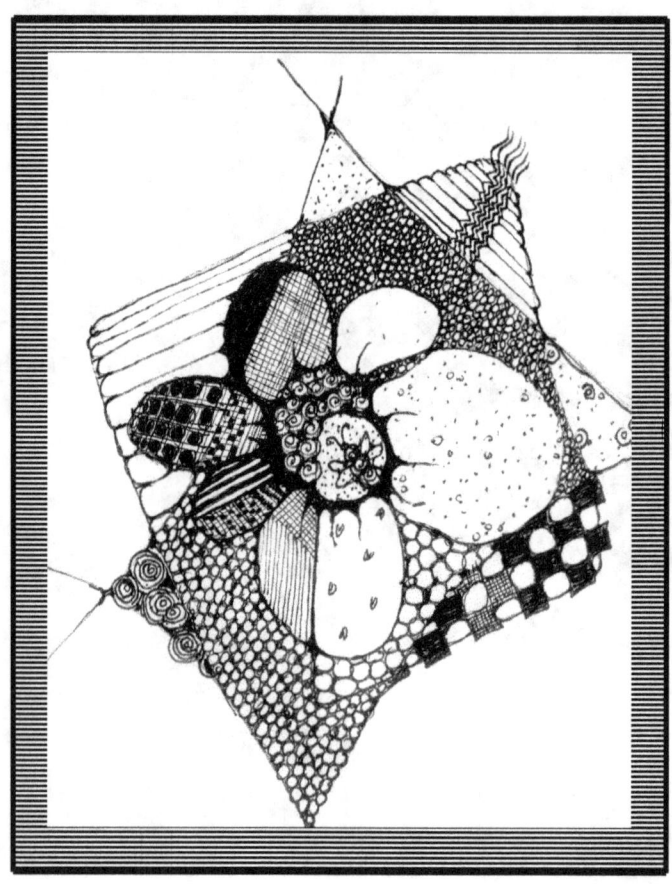

The Flower 4

The following patterns are used in NeoWhimsy Flower 4:

Dots	**Black caviar**	**Squares**
Whirles	**Red caviar**	**Lines with softened ends**
Waves	**Chess board**	**Circles in circles**

The following pages include visual instructions showing step-by-step how to create NeoWhimsy Flower 4. The easy flowing line creates the shapes-sections, and then artist fills the sections with different patterns.

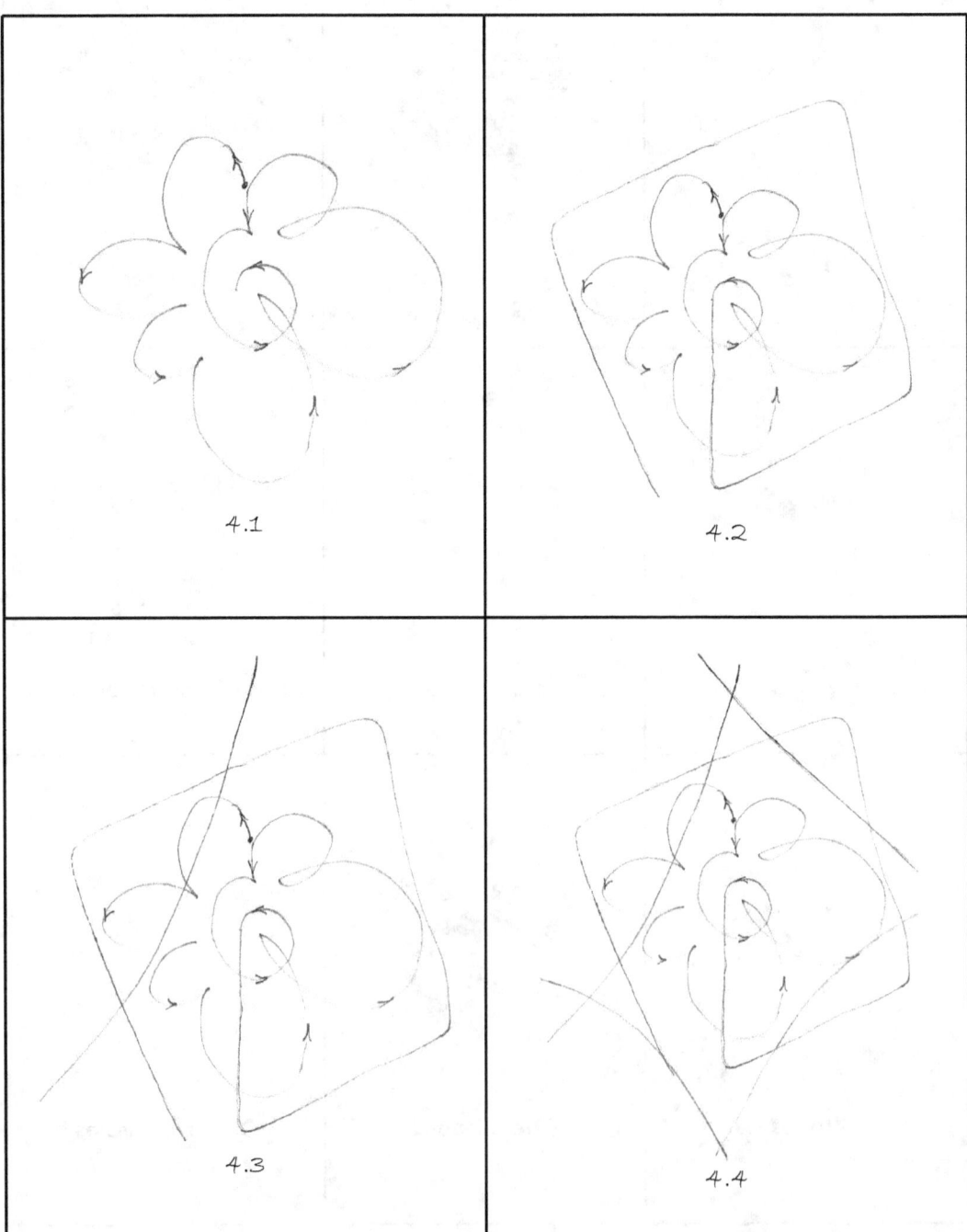

4.1

4.2

4.3

4.4

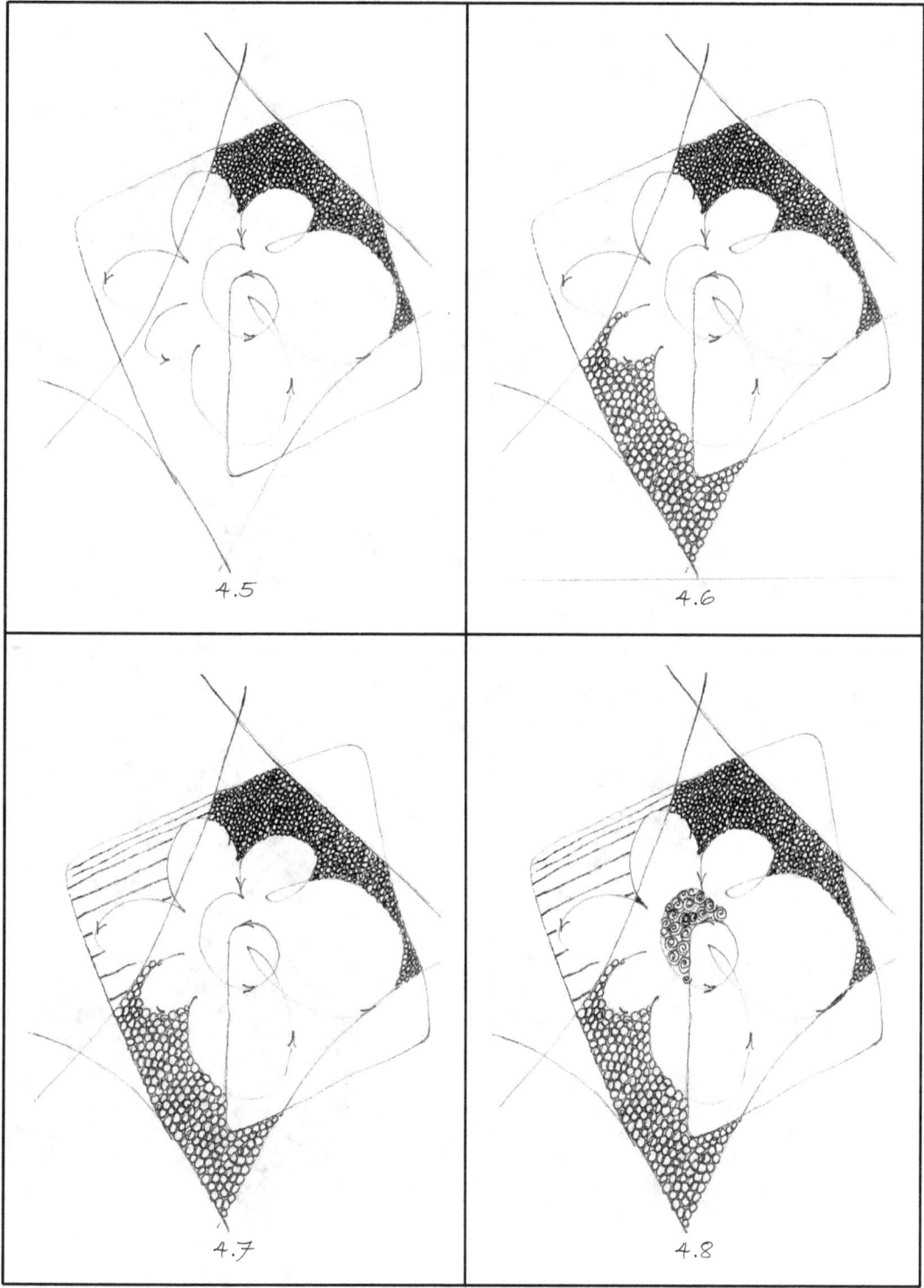

4.5

4.6

4.7

4.8

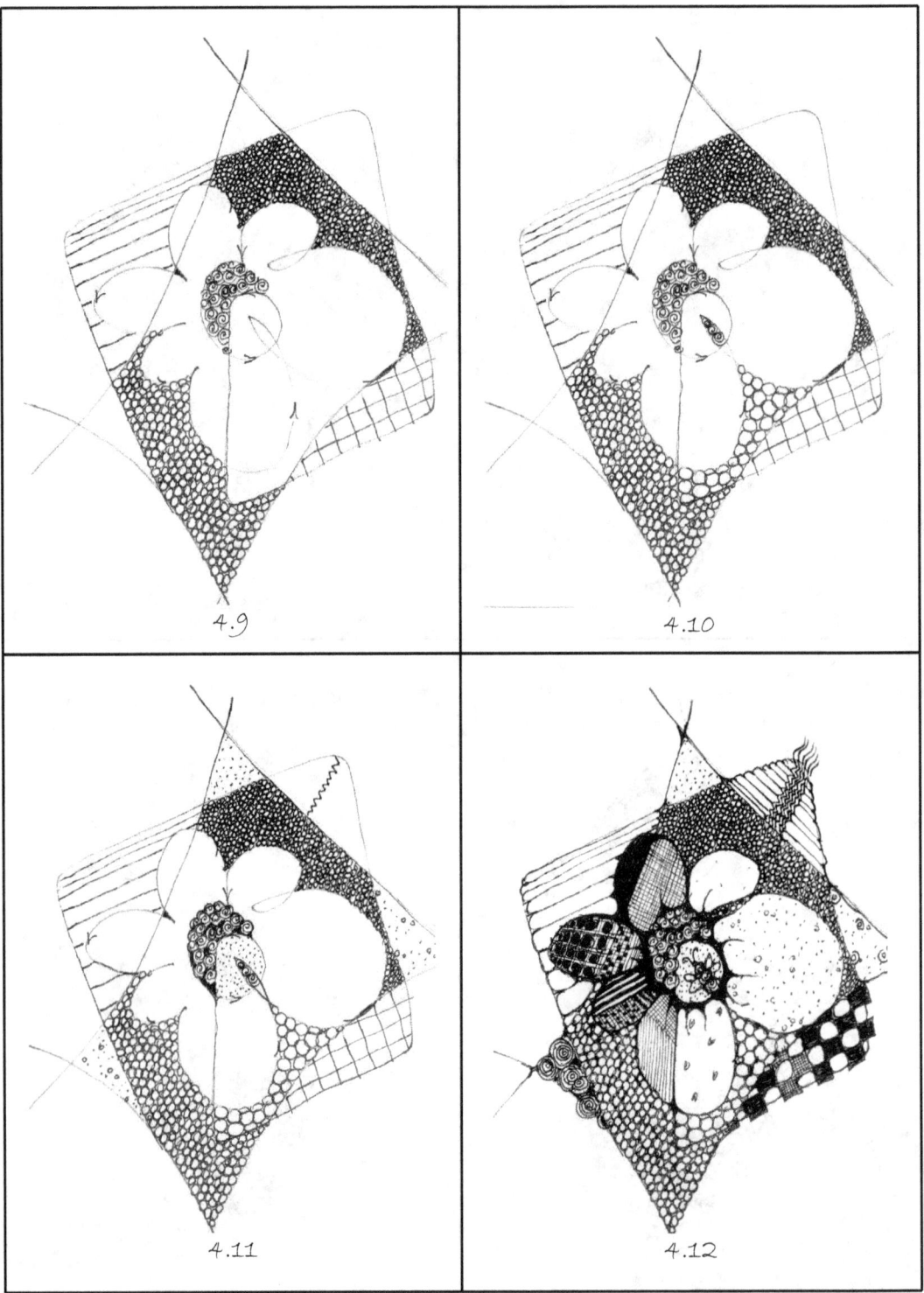

4.9

4.10

4.11

4.12

Draw the Flowers Here and Now

Complete the following NeoWhimsies, put some "meat" on the "bones". Do not copy the patterns of NeoWhimsies that you see in this book. Use your imagination, employ your skill and create absolutely new and unique drawings. Remember that imagination and inventiveness are necessary aspects of any creativity.

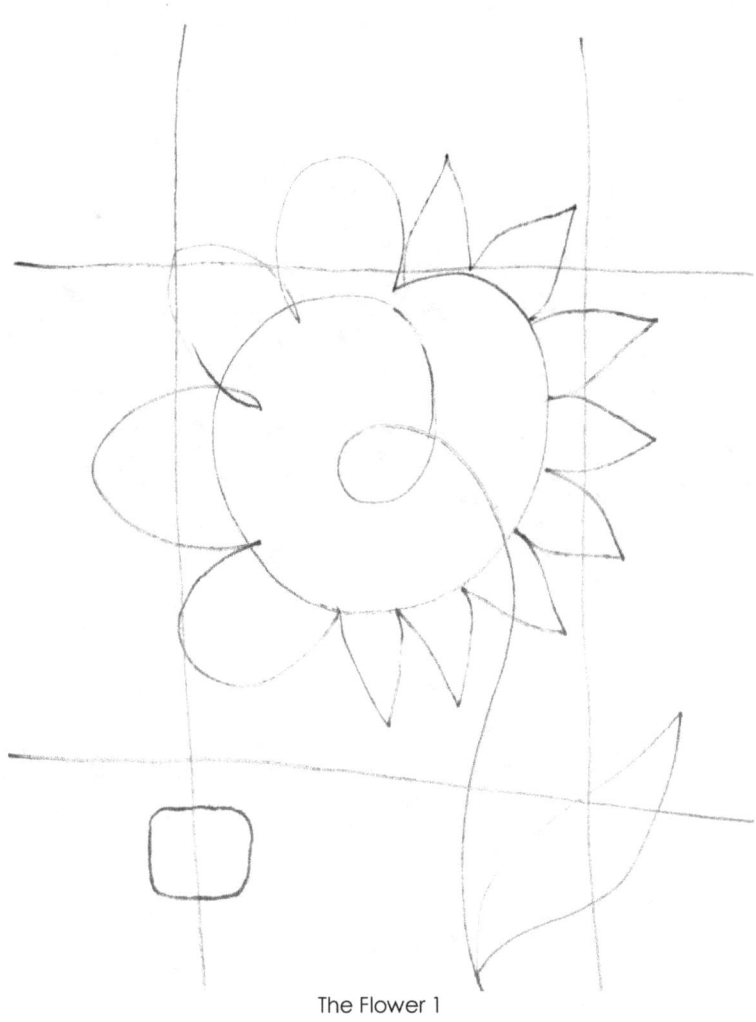

The Flower 1

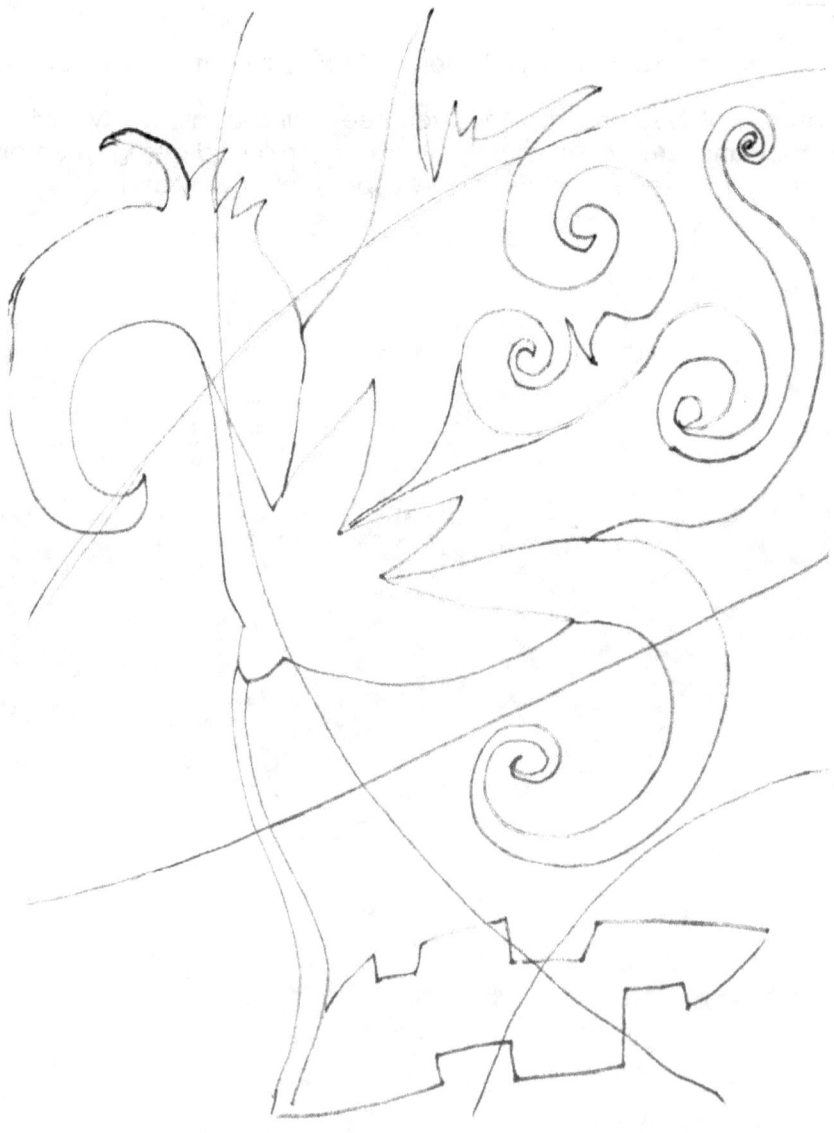

The Flower 2

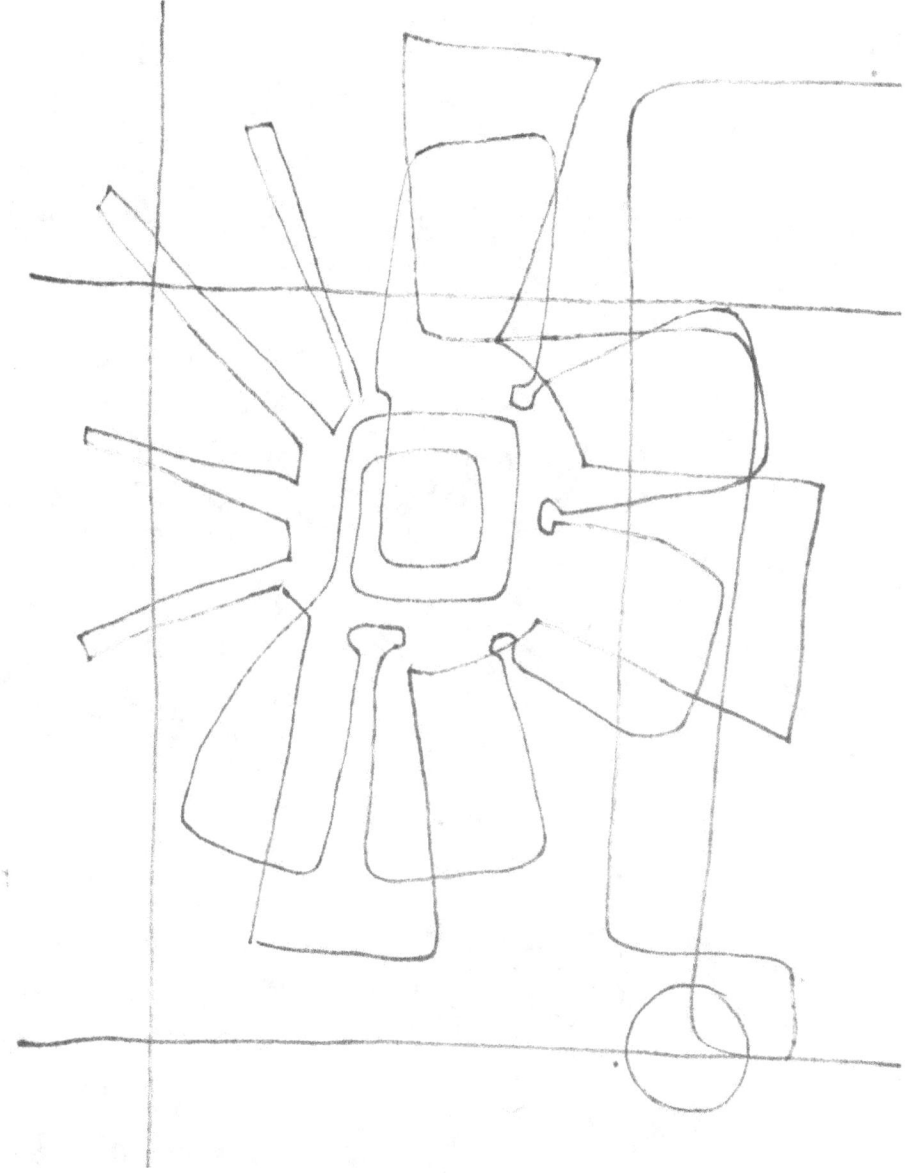

The Flower 3

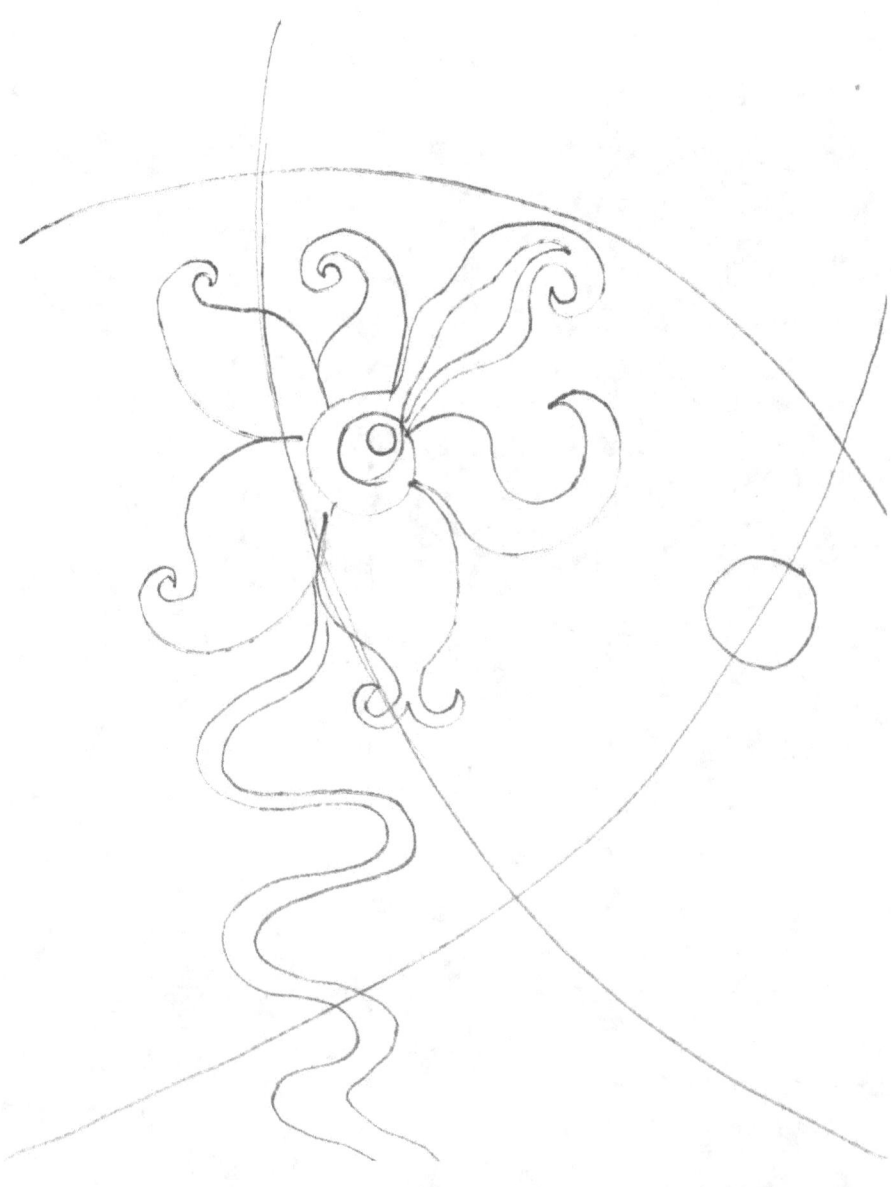

The Flower 4

Create Your NeoWhimsies from the Scratch

Use the following pages to create new NeoWhimsies. It could be the imaginative grasshoppers and flowers, umbrellas and hats, anything you like. Draw the flowing lines, fill sections with patterns. Do it with ease. Use the circle, squares, triangles, rectangular, dots, rays, "snakes", small flowers, other objects, their combinations and different variations, explore different sizes. Some sections leave blank. Use your imagination and artistic intuition. Do not forget about Syncopation. Draw your NeoWhimsies step-by-step, develop your skills. When you draw the patterns, you enter meditative state of mind, you relaxing. Have fun, create, meditate!

Draw your NeoWhimsy here.

Draw your NeoWhimsy here

■

Create Your Repetitive
Patterns Gallery

Use the following pages to create repetitive patterns Gallery. Fill each section with different imaginative ornaments - patterns. Use line, circles, squares, ovals, triangles, zigzags, rectangular, dots, other small objects, combine them. You will use these patterns later in your future NeoWhimsies. Impossible is nothing, use your imagination, develop your skills!

1	2	3
4	5	6
7	8	9

10	11	12
13	14	15
16	17	18
19	20	21

About NeoPopRealism creator NADIA RUSS

Nadia Russ (aka Nadejda Maloletneva) was born into a former professional military officer's family. As a child, she began studying art from famous masters of the past through art books and reproductions, which her mother Vera was collecting in their home. Nadia daily heard about and saw the reproductions of works of Leonardo da Vinci, Michelangelo, Rafael, contemporary Russian artists such as Petrov-Vodkin.

She began painting and drawing seriously in 1989. A few months later, her first ink drawings were exhibited in a group exhibition in famous Moscow's Manege and later, in other Moscow's art galleries. In 1992, she successfully showed her work in New York City.

In 1996-2000, Nadia resided in the Bahamas, where her work gained some special brightness. There, she got her pseudonym to her original 'Nadejda Maloletneva', which was easier to pronounce - 'Nadia Russ'. In 2000-2001, in Xanadu hotel, she operated her Art Gallery Club 13.

In 2000, she moved to the United States, where she lives up until present. January 4, 2003, Nadia Russ created a word NeoPopRealism and manifested internationally new style of visual arts which combines the brightness and simplicity of Pop Art with deep and psychological realism and has graphic nature. Her artworks are in private and permanent public collections including MOYA - Museum of Young Art in Vienna (Austria), Simferopol and Sumy Art Museums in Ukraine, Kinsey Institute of Indiana University (USA), Ukrainian Museum in New York City (USA), WEAM - World Erotic Art Museum in Miami (USA), Schacknow Museum of Fine Arts (USA), Historical Museum of Fort Lauderdale (USA), Lebedyn and Konotop Art Museums (Ukraine), D. Burliuk Foundation (Ukraine), and other.

In 2008-2010, Nadia Russ founded and juried Int'l NeoPopRealism Starz Art competitions. In 2009-2011, she authored a few art-related books such as "NeoPopRealism Starz: 21st Century ART" two volumes, "New Millennium ART", "Fort Lauderdale 100: A Must-Have Collector's Edition" three volumes, and a series of teaching/ leaning books on how to draw NeoPopRealism ink images. She is the founder (2007) of NeoPopRealism Journal & Wonderpedia, publications online, dedicated to arts, culture, books, news, celebrities and more. Nadia Russ lives in New York City and Florida. Visit her website at www.nadiaruss.com.

Conclusion

What is Art?

Now, when you know how to draw NeoPopRealism ink images - the NeoWhimsies, you might have your answer to this open question. We'd like to hear from you, e-mail us neopoprealismpress@mail.com. Also, if you have a blog, post there the images of your NeoPopRealism ink drawings and a story about how you learned to draw them. Have a wonderful journey to the world of NeoWhimsies and NeoPopRealism!

NeoPopRealism ten canons for happier life

1. Be beautiful.

2. Be creative and productive; never stop studying and learning.

3. Be peace-loving, positive-minded.

4. Do not accept totalitarian philosophy.

5. Be free-minded, do the best you can to move the world to peace and harmony.

6. Be family oriented, self-disciplined.

7. Be free spirited. Follow your dreams, if they are not destructive, but constructive.

8. Believe in god. God is one. It is harmony and striving for perfection.

9. Be supportive to those who need you, be generous.

10. Create your life as a great adventurous story.

Nadia Russ, 2004

Additional books - teaching / learning material on NeoPopRealism Ink drawing for adults, teenagers and children

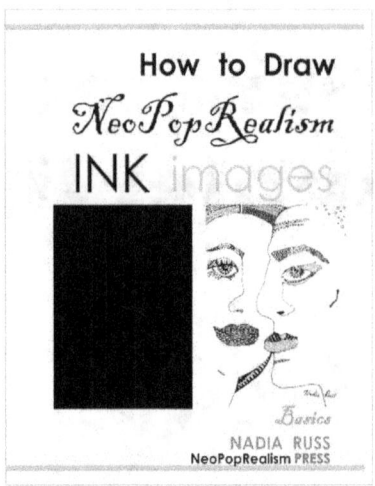

ISBN: 9780615515755
FOR TEENS & ADULTS

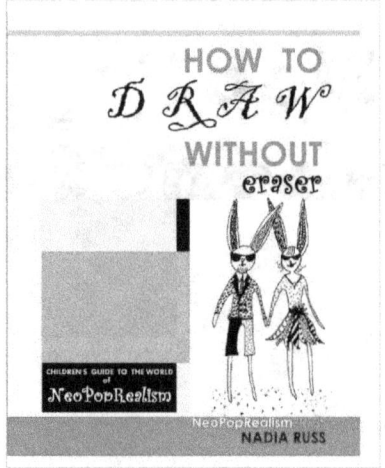

ISBN: 9780615521824
FOR CHILDREN

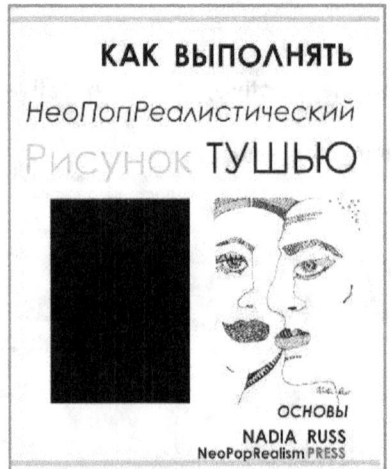

Book "*How to Draw NeoPopRealism Ink Images: Basics*" in Russian translation.
ISBN: 9780615516967

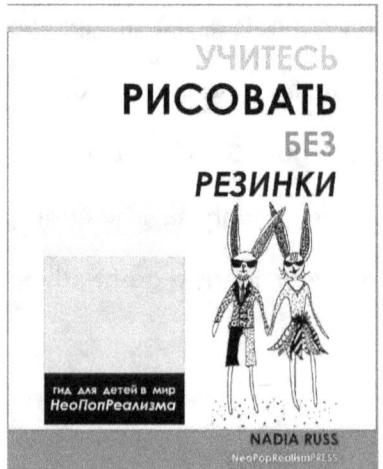

Book "*How to Draw Without Eraser: Backgrounds*" in Russian translation.
ISBN: 9780615523484

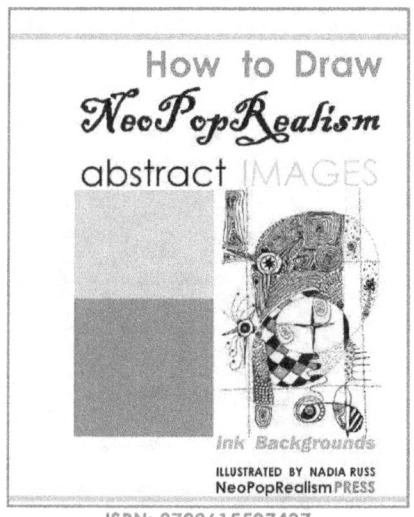

ISBN: 9780615527437
FOR TEENS & ADULTS

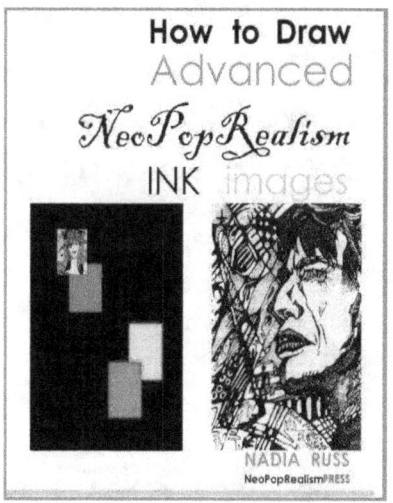

ISBN: 9780615569758
FOR TEENS & ADULTS

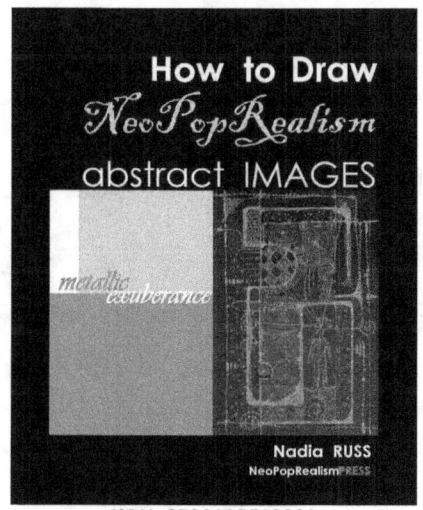

ISBN: 9780615560991
FOR TEENS & ADULTS

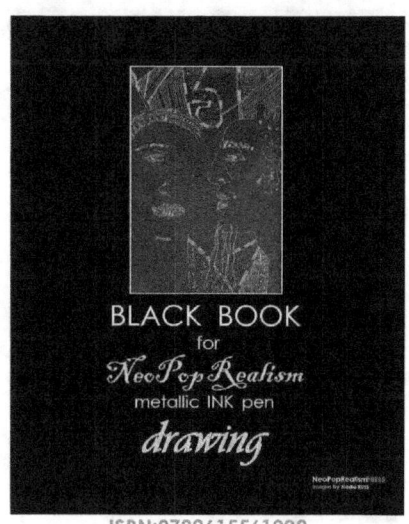

ISBN:9780615561028
FOR ALL AGES & LEVELS

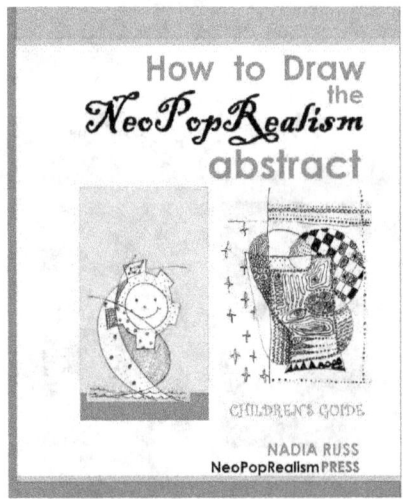

ISBN: 9780615545332

FOR CHILDREN

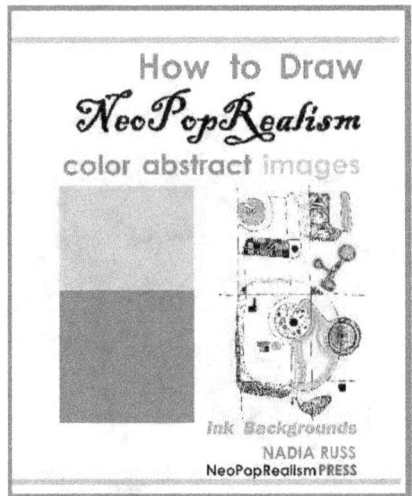

ISBN: 9780615579559

FOR TEENS & ADUTS

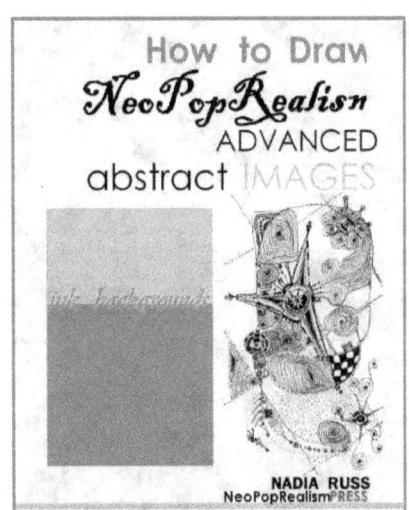

ISBN: 9780615592558

FOR TEENS & ADULTS

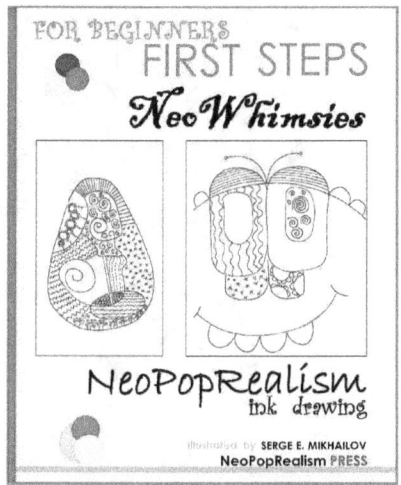

ISBN: 9780615641553
FOR CHILDREN & ARTISANS

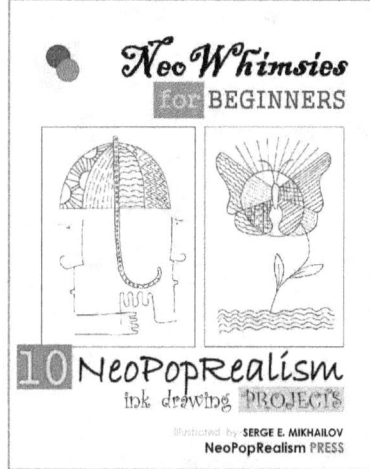

ISBN: 9780615645087
FOR CHILDREN & ARTISANS

www.ingramcontent.com/pod-product-compliance
Lightning Source LLC
Chambersburg PA
CBHW081206180526

45170CB00006B/2237